BLUE-COLLAR ACTOR

TIPS, TALES, & RECOLLECTIONS TO HELP YOU GET IN THE ACTING GAME

ANDY GUZE

This book is dedicated to Alex, Mom,
and all my fellow actors in the struggle.

BLUE-COLLAR ACTOR
Tips, Tales, & Recollections to Help You Get in the Acting Game

©2020 Andy Guze

andyguze@gmail.com

ISBN 978-0-578-57604-6 paperback
ISBN 978-0-578-57626-8 eBook
Registered with Library of Congress

Cover and Back Cover Design by Simon J. Tate
Interior Design by Tristen Jackman

Author's Photo by Adrian Baschuk

Contents

PREFACE

In the early conceptualization of this book, I was quickly daunted about how exactly to title these pages. Some writers just write, right out of the gate. Then, as the prose piles up, they give their work a title.

Others flip that. Some may score a title at some point within the process. In my experiences of writing, which up until this point has just been poetry (rap lyrics), unproduced screenplays, and Instagram captions, I like to have the title locked in before sentence one. (Cart before the horse? Guilty. You don't even know how early I got started on the cover art and I already have my outfit picked out for my first imaginary book signing!)

That's just me. A dreamer at your service. I'll be inserting quite a bit of me in these pages so it's not just some impersonal handbook. Nor is this book just a collection of memoirs relevant to the profession of acting. Rather it's a hybrid of the two, a guide of sorts, coupled with collections of insights and experiences I have amassed to hopefully help you as you set out on your journey as an actor.

In the case that you're not an actor (Hi, Mom!) and are just reading this for an unfiltered peek into this volatile career path,

I am also aiming to keep you entertained. That's an easy lay-up since this line of work is truly absent of dull moments. So regarding the title, *How To Get Started In Acting or Confessions of a Working Actor* just didn't ring right for me.

I'll surely be going off on little tangents and editorialize from time to time. I'd like to offer my pre-thanks to you for humoring me as I occasionally drift along in my stream of consciousness. Life is but a dream after all.

This book isn't to tell you how to act, but rather how to start acting, how to get in the game, navigate the game, and actually get paid for services of being in front of a camera. I have managed to do this in what one would deem a non-acting city. Miami is not considered a blue-collar town *per se*, but if you work here as an actor, you are a blue-collar actor. Translation: You'll have to refrain from keeping your nose in the air and be open to all opportunities that may arise. Because:

Work is work

My collar is blue

Money is green

Make checks payable to

If you desire to switch that collar to a lighter hue, say the lightest and whitest of all (assuming you don't already reside in LA or NYC), then you'll have to move out. That's what many actors have done and will continue to do, leaving the cities and townships they call home to pursue an ambition they call a dream. It's crap-shoot and a gamble of one's time, comforts, pride, and routine. As an actor moving to New York or LA, you're playing a hand of cards, and each of those cards not only represents your ambition, but your looks, your will, your stamina, your representation, and your luck. And destiny, she's the dealer. The only way to know if your hand is a winner is to go.

This book is for the stubborn or less fortunate. Because you don't need to go to Julliard or the Yale School of Drama to tap the well of your inner truth. You simply need to put your fabulous self out there and get started in this business as soon as possible. That is your truth, wherever you are in society or geographically.

This book is also for the hustler, looking to break into acting as a means of income, be it a side hustle, or an actual main hustle. Perhaps you've seen a commercial or have noticed a film set in your town and you wondered how much these actors were making. You're intrigued about the possibility of becoming an actor yourself.

I am a little bit of both of these. I'm a stubborn hustler and perhaps that is what has kept me un-famous and underappreciated, and I'm ok with that. Really. And until Hollywood or NYC summons me, hungry for the multitude of my talents, I will contently remain a blue-collar actor here, in the old 305, with the AC on blast.

REWIND

"The creative adult is the child who survived."

— Julian F. Fleron

Off the bat, let us rewind back to the roots of our passion. Why do you want be an actor? When did you know? My passion for acting is rooted in my love of the movies of my childhood which took place back in the 1980's. They were the raddest of times, awesomest of times, the weirdest of times. An era when the kettle of Hollywood was popping out original gems on the grandest of scale, from the likes of *Back to the Future* to *Raiders of the Lost Ark* to *Ghostbusters*—from the theaters to the video rental store to our VHS players.

My family's extraordinary little VCR was a lionized contraption in our house, a necessity, up there with the refrigerator, the water heater, and the roof over our heads. Prior to my Miami teenage years, I lived in The Land of 10,000 Lakes' biggest city, Minneapolis. And since the brutality of those Minnesota winters kept us indoors, we'd binge on movies that kept our snowbound imaginations occupied.

Before the ease of applying a little thumb pressure to stream pretty much any movie as we do nowadays, the video rental store was the main supplier after a title's theatrical release. Less convenient undoubtedly, but more romantic by far. Along the walls of the video stores were rows and rows of little boxes, tangible promises for the taking, each cover more compelling or more ridiculous than the next. Back then, you could actually hold them in your hand, examining, turning them around, wondering, considering, gaining closer on that fateful selection of taking a movie home. But, better pick a good one, since it was all you had for two days. That is, if you didn't want a late fee. I would most likely watch them twice, maybe even three times. It was ritualistic. Movies were more than welcome at our home. And if they were good, they became part of the family. This is how it all began. Just a kid and his tightly-knit family, on a soft sofa, with a soft spot for movies, riding out cold winters.

As I matured, I began to imagine life as a working adult. People actually manufacture magic, I thought. I wanted to do that. Although in what capacity had yet to be determined.

Fast-forward some time to where my journey in self-discovery as an actor began. The year was 2000 on the dot. I was attending a film school at a little degree mill in Orlando, FL by the name of Full Sail University. There I was mostly taught the technical craft of film and TV production. That is obviously the opposite side of the camera that an actor would be interested in. Still, it was in college that I was first able to work with actors, and really observe what they did. We, a ragtag group of film students, took turns directing them. I was instantly impressed with the actors and how they moved, spoke, and performed. I kinda wanted to be them—to know what it felt like to breathe life into a character on the page of screenplay. But I suppressed the urge and didn't act on it, so to speak. For me, at least, acting at the time seemed like such a leap, such a departure from my comforts. Was I really that great enough? Who did I think I was? A subject worthy enough that a camera should record and immortalize forever? I finished the film program in December of 2001 and stayed the course as an aspiring writer-director.

Fresh out of school, I returned home, which was then and still is the tropical metropolis of Miami. In the early 2000's, there was a film production tax credit in the state of Florida (Bring it back!) and you could say that the entertainment business was booming.

But simply having a love of cinema and a film school diploma did not mean you were instantly going to be at the helm of a production, wearing black-rimmed glasses, barking orders at a trusty AD, and dating young starlets. Oh no, there is no fast track—nepotism aside. One must make their own track like the Drake track, starting from the bottom. Which I did, literally as an entry level PA (production assistant). It's very difficult to make a living as a PA; the hours are long, and the work is grueling. The production assistant is the first to show up to set and the last to leave—and earns the smallest paycheck.

I remember working on a set for a major soft drink commercial. The main actor was around my age. When he wasn't hamming it up for the camera, he was drinking coffee, smoking cigarettes, sitting in the shade, being delivered freshly blended smoothies, chatting it up with the extras, and talking to various people above and below the line. He was chillin' like a villain. He was having fun.

What a great job I thought. I asked the production coordinator how much the actor was making. It was fifteen grand. What!?

Here I am, busting my ass, making $175 for 12 hours of work and this actor is making 15 stacks for a day's "work." All that loot just to pretend he's thirsty then sell the satisfaction after taking a gulp of some sugar-loaded soda. It was then that I realized I wanted to do that.

At that point, however, I didn't have the *cojones* to give it a shot. I was just a slave-wage PA still living at home, which blew harder than a late summer tropical depression. But the arrangement allowed me the luxury to cultivate my glimmering dreams of being a director.

Around 2002, after a year in the real world, I produced a short film, *A Life in a Day*, a little symbolism-laden tale that I had whipped up back in my college screenwriting class. I assumed the role of the leading man. My first real acting gig you could say, although I was just testing the waters. As is commonly the case for first-time indie productions, I wore several hats on that shoot. From writer to director to wardrobe to locations, my talents were spread thin. I was no Orson Welles in my early 20's. I didn't truly feel as if I was acting back then. It felt as if I was just completing a task. Just like booking a location or choosing an outfit for a scene. Although it was fun all around and it actually was premiered at the Made in Miami Film Festival (now defunct), what I took from that project was that I am not a multi-tasker. And my strengths undoubtedly are cut from the creative cloth, not the technical.

Aside from the film festival, *Life in a Day*, like 99% of independent films, went nowhere. Speaking of going nowhere, I flexed my writing chops further, penning two feature-length screenplays. I sent out query letters to literary agents in LA and NY. Surely,

I thought, they'll be interested in an unproven writer's spec script about a rejected and heartbroken young man who becomes a pimp to pay back a debt to a black-market diamond ring dealer. Yeah, no. Citizen Lame.

The reality was that I needed to make money. The PA gigs just weren't cutting it. It's now around 2005, the height of the Reality TV era. Reality TV is a producer's dream come true. No need for real actors, which means rock-bottom rates for talent (sometimes free) and cheap production value, keeping the crews lean. MTV onboarded me as a casting associate to help populate their dating shows with young faces eager for their 15 minutes. I got a pretty good rate and a fat per diem. I, along with the casting team, was sent on the road, setting up shop in various American cities. My duties consisted of partying with college kids, inviting them to try out for an MTV show, and then shooting their casting tapes for the producers back in NY. As a single 25-year-old fellow with a good head of hair, there were worse jobs out there. But was this what I really wanted to do? You can't cast college kids forever.

Fast-forward three years, after a whirlwind of casting hundreds of dudes and dudettes. I was amassing thousands of Myspace friends, and even taking up residence in NYC for a stint. But then I returned home to the city of humidity. The Reality TV experience was over. But the reality was this really wasn't me and wasn't what I ultimately wanted to do. Still, I casted on.

With all this Reality TV casting experience, I was able to land a few more jobs in that wheelhouse. Although maturing as an artist, it felt less and less fulfilling. There was always that sense that I'm not the only one that can do this. I could be anyone. If I wasn't able to do what I truly wanted in this industry, maybe I'll just leave it all together. And I did...temporarily.

So in addition for film and TV, I've always had a love affair for fashion. Maybe it's in my DNA. I am, after all, the product of a retail romance. My parents met while working at a department store, the flagship Macy's in Herald Square in New York City. Fast-forward to their son in his late 20's as he gives up on his film and tv aspirations. Suppress one passion and watch another bubble right up. As an observer and practitioner of fashion and branding, I went ahead and started what was initially a men's clothing line for the college sports market. I called the line Flying Colors Apparel and was very fortunate to entice a couple of investors who helped me get things off the ground.

I was now a fashion designer. That meant studying cutting-edge trends from the taste-making runways, mocking up silhouettes and cads, and slapping together collections. The company and I saw some success with sales, with the men's line, but we soon understood that we would have to target the ladies if we really wanted to ramp up our numbers. So, I produced and starred in these marketing videos for YouTube called Girls Gone Styled. The concept was cute. Instead of college girls taking their tops off a la spring break Girls Gone Wild, the camera man and I would hit the college tailgate parties and have them put on the tops from my line!

Put it on, girl! And put in on they did. Similar to my MTV days, I was on the road, another American collegiate odyssey from UF to FSU to Texas Tech to ASU. It was fun, creating clothes and marketing schemes, giving out the next spirited shirt to the next gracious girl next door. But the real enjoyment was what I missed and what I wanted: the camera and its capture. And I knew I couldn't make silly little Girls Gone Styled videos forever. The Flying Colors team had a good run. The effort to target the fairer sex proved victorious, so much so we were granted more team licenses. Sales went up by 50% and the line shifted solely for the ladies. The logo was changed to appear more feminine and the men's pieces I designed were cancelled. After three years, I didn't really even recognize this brand that I initially started. And sure enough, that restlessness of an artist kicked in and I wanted to leave the company. It turns out I don't bleed college fashion. I struck a deal with the partners and walked. Walked where was the question.

There I was again, at a juncture in life. With uncertainty in high gear, one radiant Miami winter morning I was driving down Biscayne Boulevard...

INT/EXT. ANDY'S CAR / BISCAYNE BOULEVARD – MORNING

The rising sun creeps over the bay. ANDY, mid 20's, determined eyes, interested in life and optimistic. Behind the wheel of a decrepit Toyota, he slows down as he nears a barricade in the middle of the road. A COP waves him to detour.

> **ANDY**
>
> Good morning, Officer.

Andy looks beyond the barricade, noticing that it's a film set.

> **OFFICER**
>
> Go that way.

> **ANDY**
>
> What are they shooting here?

> **OFFICER**
>
> Did I stutter? Keep it moving!

Andy obeys, turning off the boulevard onto the side street.

INT/EXT. ANDY'S CAR / DOWNTOWN SIDE STREET - MOMENTS LATER

Andy busts a quick U-turn and slowly drives back toward the boulevard, getting a vantage point of the film set. Just out of the Officer's view.

Andy puts the car in park, lights up a cigarette, and observes.

                    ANDY
      Damn, I gotta get back on set.

He sits smoking, while observing the camera on
dolly tracks, the grips, the trailers, the props,
craft services, the PA's, the producers, the director, the extras, and THE ACTORS. Andy comes
to a decision and his eyes light up. He stubs
out His cigarette in the car ashtray, and then
smirks.

                   ANDY (VO)
    But, this time it's going to be different.
                   This time…

Andy looks at Himself in the rearview mirror and
says to himself:
                    ANDY
        I'm going to be a fucking actor.

                              FADE OUT:

Why the digression? Why did I just drag you through a con-
densed version of my life—my highlight reel, in actor terminol-
ogy—before I really decided to become an actor? Because the
road of an actor is rough one, full of peaks, plateaus, and valleys.
The setbacks are a given, and you have to be ready—even if you're
never ready. So saddle up and hold on tight to the roots of your
passion, never losing sight of the romance that lead you into this
crazy business to begin with.

After all that time, after a decade-plus of odd production jobs, and entrepreneurial endeavors, I finally came to terms with what I really wanted to do. My longtime passion collided with purpose and will. For some of you, this may have come easy; the proverbial acting bug bit and in turn you began your journey as an actor. You laced up your Nikes and just did it. For others, to act on their aspirations, it's not that easy. Because there are always challenges. Certain circumstances, expectations of those around us, and even self-doubt make it difficult to take cues from our inner voice and follow a passion. But eventually, inevitably, naturally, rightfully, hopefully we succumb to what it is we love to do.

For me, acting was no longer an aspiration, but a destiny. It was a goal that I set out to do, just as you are right now. So without further ado, congrats to you! Because you have made the decision to act on your aspirations. It is now a matter of owning it.

Take a look in the mirror—or reverse that camera on your iPhone—and say the following words loudly and confidently: I am an actor. Repeat this until it feels comfortable. Saying it to yourself is the easy part, of course, but telling the universe not so much. But that is the groundwork to becoming. And this book will help you arrive at this step with confidence and conviction.

Once you are doing, you officially are. You are an actor.

"To do is to be."
—Nietzsche

GET LEGIT

"You got any idea what my life would be
worth if certain people found out I checked
into a laughing academy?"
— Tony Soprano

"Don't quit your day job." It's a favorite go-to phrase that haters like to lay on you when you express your career ambition or show your talents as a performer. Well, I am here to tell, to do just that: quit your day job. Once you have made all the moves needed, you'll need to quit that day job for several reasons that I will lay out in this chapter. And as far as the haters go, that just goes with the territory. The more you progress, the more you'll win over—or push away—those pesky little fuckers. It is a fact of life. But once you hit it big, those pests will be contrasted by fans. Lots of them. Little fuckers, begone! Ignore them and keep grinding away at attaining your dream.

A *Day Job* is full-time—as in a 9-5 job. The kind of work that monopolizes the majority of one's life, leaving just a fraction of free time to do whatever it is they do outside of work. This day job is not to be confused with a side-hustle, although a side-hustle is key when getting the ball rolling as an actor.

I remember when I was starting out and my agent would send me out to castings. Castings are full of people like you, patiently waiting for the opportunity to be seen and given the opportunity to do their thing and live their dream, People at casting calls would wait sometimes hours for their audition.

Is this all they do, I would ponder. Are all these people full-time actors that can afford to take off an entire afternoon to wait around in a casting director's office? Do they have day jobs or side-hustles? The answer to that last question is yes. Most actors, artists for that matter, can't 100% live from their craft, so they have other jobs. Of course this doesn't pertain to you if you are independently wealthy or have some kind of passive revenue stream. Must be nice! Can I borrow a dollar a million times over? For the rest of us common yet uncommon, folk, we'll be needing another job to subsidize the life of an actor, to tread the murky waters of capitalism.

And with great emphasis, I will tell you that it is key that this other job is flexible, because this acting business is all about being available. You are essentially your agent's product. They are trying to sell you to the casting directors who are trying to sell you to the producers and director. When your agent sends you to an audition, it is typically with short to no notice. Sometimes your presence is requested the very next day or even that very day. And you seldom get to reschedule.

And then when you've impressed the gatekeepers, the powers that be, and the producers want to actually book you, you better be available to work. Like, right away. If not, you'll start to get a rep as unreliable. This is a deal-breaker in this industry. Your agent will drop you faster than you can say "Did I get the part?"

So let's say the Acting Gods (I will address the Acting Gods more fully in a later chapter) were with you and you did indeed get the part. Mazel Tov! Now, depending on the scale of the job, things get busy.

They are going to have a fitting for wardrobe, typically within 48 hours of being booked on the job. Fittings can last hours. Then the production will email you a call sheet, at which point you will see what time you are to report to set. This is known as the call time. There is no rescheduling a call time. Your call time is a command; it might as well be etched in stone. So again, an actor's life must be flexible. I'm talking Cirque du Soleil flexible.

I'm in no way a vocational expert. If I were a high school guidance counselor, I would instruct all my kids to simply follow their teenage hearts forever. But, between acting gigs—and there will be spaces between gigs – you need to find a back-up job. Something that is flexible and allows you to drop it in a hot minute if an acting gig comes up. It's called survival. Here are a few flexible jobs that I know of. Some of them my acting friends have actually held down these part-time careers between jobs.

Real Estate Agent
This I found, at least in South Florida, is by far the most common job people take on. It is very flexible. But it is commission-based so, like the acting game, you are only as good as your last hit.

Bartender
Also great for networking. You never know who may belly-up to your bar. Just try to keep your personal booze intake at a low, since you'll be needing your days to shine as an actor on the grind. A tequila on the rocks, splash of water, and tons of lime wedges, please!

Personal Trainer/Yoga/Pilates
For all you bona fide fit girls and guys, i.e. freaks. Keep your killer bod in tip-top shape while awaiting that callback. Stay flexible on the yoga mat and on the calendar.

Video Editor
Whether you're cutting up reels for your actor friends or even wedding videos for newlyweds, this occupation can serve you well. Maybe you don't have any post-production skills, but like anything, it can be learned and is fairly easy—especially now with iMovie.

Salesman
If you're a gun-for-hire, a commission-based sales person, then you are the master of your destiny. That is, your destiny of dollars. Akin to acting, you eat what you kill. If you kill often enough, you'll in turn have time to kill for your auditions. Like Alec Baldwin famously commands in Glengarry Glen Ross, "Always Be Closing."

Rideshare Driver
I actually drove for Uber when it was first introduced in Miami. During my ascension as a working actor, I was able to cover my expenses by driving people all over. That way, all the acting jobs income I landed were icing on the cake. Five stars!

And the list goes on. Chances are, as an aspiring artist, you're not exactly Warren Buffet when it comes to handling your finances. But you'll need to take the time to assess your income situation and have a financial game plan. I would defer you to my guy Sos Talks Money (Google him) on this. Yes, I am saying to quit your day-job and get a solid side-hustle. But only quit when you're 100% prepared for success. MC Hammer famously said, "Too legit to quit." In the case of an actor on the rise, I'd like to rephrase that: "Get legit to quit!"

How does one get legit, you ask? You must get those proverbial ducks in a row, so read on.

HEADSHOT

"A picture is worth a thousand words.
A headshot is worth a thousand rejections."

— Unknown

A headshot is the paramount preamble to a career as an actor. It is you kicking into action, the first step that is to say, *This is really happening; I am an aspiring actor.*

A headshot is an actor's calling card, the face of your personal brand, the beacon by which you will initially be judged, considered, discarded, and in due time, invited to an audition and, sooner or later, booked on your first gig. Before the credits, before the agent, before the reel, as Mia Wallace (from *Pulp Fiction*) needed an adrenaline shot to her chest, you will need a headshot.

Speaking of Tarantino, the king of smart crime sagas, headshots are very much like mugshots. The only difference is the person in the headshot photo actually wants to be booked. Yet, like thugs and criminals, us actors are on the outskirts of society, rolling the dice in the casino of life, against all odds. The stakes are similar; where failure for a criminal could be the state penitentiary, for an actor it's a day job. Both are in the clink.

Sometimes a headshot is the beginning and the end. Temporarily, for me at least.

Recall back in the first chapter where I hastily dragged you through my life, prior to deciding to wholeheartedly to become an actor? I failed to mention many things. Like around the time I produced my short film, which I also acted in, circa 2002, I was really feeling myself. So I went ahead and hired one of Miami's best headshot takers to fire off some stills of your boy here.

Ah, the early 21st century. In those days, our cell phones were stupid and flipped. Real photos were taken by headshot photographers. They actually shot aspiring actors and actresses on a medium called film. And it was the industry trend to shoot this film in classic black and white. My photo session was awkward. Rather than hold a pose, I would start to act. Like, in motion. Without a movie camera. That's not cool when a photo is known as a "still." To this day, when I'm having stills taken, it's still a big fail for me. I can't freeze in my pose. That day, it meant a lot of wasted time and wasted films. In these digital days, it just means wasted time. Take my advice and don't develop this tic. Really.

After the photo session, I had to wait days before the photographer presented me with a contact sheet, another relic of the past. She circled her selects of the best shots for my review. Now I have been photographed since the dawn of my life, but this was different. These shots were professional. It was a weird exercise of ego. The complete amateur, I was looking at a photo series of some aspiring star, an alterna-version of me donning various poses and looks. These shots could've been in a *Vanity Fair* article. Am I really doing this? I thought.

After I chose the winning shot, there was more waiting as the photographer worked in her darkroom with chemicals to create my all-star close-up. Eventually, she texted me on my Nextel phone with the awesome news: the master shot was ready to be sent to the printers.

Strike a pose then pick a pose. My first session of headshots on film.

Then more waiting. It was another week or so before I finally picked up the box. Inside lay a hundred headshots bearing my young face. To rise to the occasion, nervously, I had donned a gaze of snarky confidence. That self-conscious gaze for the camera was far from the truth. It more represented where I wanted to be.

Aside from the one headshot that my mom gave to my grandmother, which hangs in her bedroom to this day, the box of headshots ended up in my closet. There they collected dust, while years flew by. I eventually collected enough confidence to go forward, desperately but courageously attending auditions with a resume and headshot in hand.

Since then I have only had one more real headshot taken—ten years ago. I am actually quite embarrassed to say that I have used the same headshot for a decade. Talk about the #10 Year Challenge! This is truly unprofessional; just ask my agents. But every casting director in my city knows me already, so they don't even look at the headshot as this point. And as far as booking di-

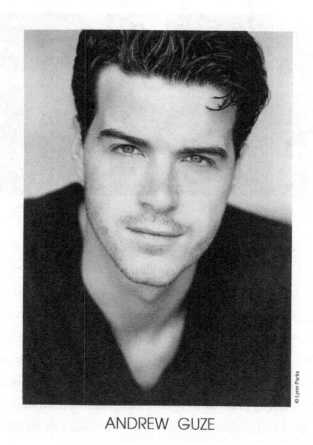

ANDREW GUZE

Never forget your first headshot (rookie card). By Lynn Parks Circa 2002

rectly to a client, they're (hopefully) looking at my experience-laden reel or a video submission.

Keep in mind, nobody is going to say: "Hey we loved your audition, you nailed it, but we just don't care too much for your headshot." But when you are starting out in the business—which is why you picked up this book—make no mistake; a good headshot can get you in the door.

When you're just starting out, you'll want that headshot to look just like you. Not younger, not older, not cooler, not hotter. But a total reflection of the real you; not just a passing resemblance. If you have a dorkiness to you, that should be come across in the shot. If you're shooting for villain roles, you better look like a mean motherfucker in your headshot. Play to your strengths and flex your quirks. I repeat: Play to your strengths and flex your quirks. Warning: I may drop that phrase again and again to the point that it's tatted on the left side of your brain.

Are you planning on focusing on film and TV or commercials? My advice, if you want to line your pockets deeply and greenly and swiftly, is to focus on everything—well except Reality TV and porn. Of course, if you're trying to become a reality star, then you should stop reading and burn this book right now. Then make a porn, preferably in the vein of a spontaneous home movie a la Kim K or Paris H. Be somebody after fucking somebody. That's one way to attain fame. Fleeting fame. Probably a lot less than those proverbial 15 minutes of fame you dream of.

Seriously, if you want to work as much as possible, you'll want to get two headshots made. One for the commercial market, that suggests you're just a basic bitch. You know, relatable with a twist of aspirational. You're the girl or boy next door that can smile on command and hawk anything under the sun.

The second headshot is for the film and TV world. Recalling my aforementioned statement to play to your strengths and flex your quirks, it's probably best to ask yourself a powerful question: Who are you? Next question: Who would the audience perceive you as? This headshot should hit the sweet spot, somewhere where self-awareness meets external perception. Know which type you are. There can be wiggle room. But consistency in character is a good goal when you are starting out and casting agents are just getting to know you.

Your headshot should be shot by a professional on a professional camera. No iPhones. I am no photographer, but I know a bad headshot when I see one, and so does everyone else in the industry. If you can't afford a professional photographer, ask your friend with the dslr camera (we all have one) to fire off some shots in the natural sunlight so it fills your face. Work that camera, baby; After the shooter has fired off a few dozen shots. Then ask your agent, if you have one at this point, to help in selecting the perfect headshot for both the commercial and film, TV, and commercial markets.

OWN THY SELF

"Today you are YOU, that is truer than true.
There is NO ONE alive that is more
YOUER than YOU!"
— Dr. Seuss

You are you. Fact. Embrace that. I also happen to be me. She is she and he is he and so on and so forth. (John Lennon was the Walrus). There are no two humans alike. Our facial features and hair color, the pitch of our voices, our mannerisms, our heights, our widths, our beauty, our flaws, our jaws, etc., are all unique attributes, exclusive to our respective selves. Also socially, culturally, and geographically we vastly differ from the majority of the people in the world. We may not be perfect, but we are perfectly us, as individuals. We are all exotic. Work that individuality!

I have been deemed handsome on occasion. Hey, I'll take it. Absolutely. Good grooming, exercise, and a diet are partly be responsible for this physical fortitude. Genes are the other reason. Now, Mr. Guze wasn't really there while I was growing up, but even an absent father can pass on traits. My blue eyes, dark brown hair, fair skin tone, and height are all courtesy of my father's Guze family genes. I also inherited his mannerisms, quirky ways, and even some of his particular interests. We are both creatures of comfort and share a fondness for shoes, politics, history, New York City, and old radios. You could say, overall, I pretty much turned out ok, physically speaking. Thanks, Dad.

So that's why I am just perfect. Oh, there this one complaint. Actually there's quite a few in fact, of a dermatological nature. Ever since puberty, I've been collecting more skin issues than a dirty magazine rack. At this point I'm fucking riddled with them. They are indelible imperfections, unflattering flaws that plague various parts of my body. So let's list them, shall we? In no particular order, I have and or have had: folliculitis, chronic acne, cystic acne (huge mounds of pus and blood growing under the surface of my face), pockmarks, keloid scars, scars, alopecia, oily skin, and the legendary skin condition that plagued the late King of Pop, vitiligo.

Whew, I think I got it all. Should the acting work dry up and I'm truly hard up for cash, I could sell my (living) body to science, to be studied as a dermatological anomaly at a prestigious medical institution.

Now, understand, this is my skin we're talking about—the very thing that an actor should be comfortable in. And back when I was hesitant with the idea of getting into acting, my numerous skin issues only furthered my reluctance to jump into the acting game. It took some maturing on my part, i.e. giving less and less a fuck, before I gained the requisite confidence to become part of an industry where appearance is at least 50% of the equation.

As my collegiate youth faded, there was good news: my acne kinda cleared up. That helped me to ball up the festering caution I'd amassed and throw it all directly into the wind. It finally occurred to me that we all have "flaws;" it's what makes us human. Own it. Accept it. If you are perfect, you are not human. Go back to your planet.

I think I have a mediocre smile. And this is even after getting a gingivectomy, a dental surgery where they slice your gums to expose more teeth. I was graced with a set of white teeth. Mind you, not freakishly movie-star white, not the level of white you find on the cover of magazines, but a natural brush-my-teeth-twice-a-day white. Just an average white set of teeth isn't the best look for an actor. Teeth are a big deal. A smile can go the distance, especially in commercials. At least half of the casting breakdowns I get from my agents specify: *Must have great smile*. For about two years I would attend these castings, knowing damn well I didn't have a great smile. And for two years I never landed one those "great smile" gigs. Now I simply and wisely forgo those opportunities. I am not the great smile guy. But what I lack in pearly whites I make up for in talent. I'm a well-suited contender for that category of *"must be great actor"* guy.

I can also say with confidence, I am not the *"must have great hands"* guy. That is thanks to some pesky patches of vitiligo and a scar across my left index finger knuckle—self-inflicted with a Leatherman while working as a PA many moons over Miami ago. Nor am I the beach bod guy. For I adore pizza way too much for that. And the keloidal scar that I had mentioned is smack dab in the middle of my chest, like a bullseye of shame. So *"must look good shirtless"* in the casting breakdown is also a red flag for me.

There was that afternoon though. I dropped in a casting for a Trip Advisor commercial that, to my surprise, required a shirtless guy. At first I was just gonna turn right around and leave, but hey, I was already there.

The action of the audition was simple enough. I would take my shirt off, sit in a lounge chair with my hands behind my head, and just pretend to enjoy the beach. This is one of my specialties as I have been booked several times where some variation of this was done in the audition. It's a common request, actually. Commercials are selling you something, so showcasing people in a happy, leisurely state, is an effective selling tool. My agent called the next day. By some miracle, I managed to win over the casting director and client. I had been booked. "What, even with my scar I?" I asked in shock. "Yes," she replied brightly, "your scar is booked too!"

When I arrived on set I immediately informed the makeup man of the keloid challenge ahead. He assured me it was nothing, and caked on some foundation. They shot me shirtless, all day. The director seemed pleased as did the clients. I was confused. Are they just not seeing this lump protruding from my cleavage? Or was I just that damned good that they could live with it?

Bottom line, aspiring actors: Don't let your imperfections set you back or discourage you. Hey, people with scars want deals on travel too. On the flip side of this coin, be a realist. Don't waste precious time attending auditions that you have not a chance in hell of booking. Just know both your strengths and weaknesses and operate accordingly. But when you're just getting into the acting game, go for broke. You'll want to attend every casting. Show your agency that you're in it to win it. And show casting directors that you exist and are absolutely the best you that you can be.

My scar and I grace the national TV airwaves for Trip Advisor

CLASS ACT

"All the world's a stage, and all the
men and women merely players..."
— William Shakespeare
As You Like It

As humans, we are all actors. I really believe that. I'm not alone in this sentiment. As seen in the quote I sparked the chapter off with. Old Billy Shakespeare knew a thing or two about people, drama, and the interactions thereof. Life is a goddamned stage; we are continually performing. That is to say, acting is an innate mechanism prescribed to every human as we carry on in our day-to-day social lives. Sociologist Erving Goffman went real deep on this theory in his book *The Presentation of Self in Everyday Life*. He suggests that "We are all just actors trying to control and manage our public image; we act based on how others might see us."

Makes sense; I have a different persona dealing with a police officer than, say, my old college roommate. My style of self-presentation varies from person to person, from situation to situation. Goffman took it even further, saying we don't possess a true self. Ouch! As an artist, that one hurts.

We all have lied at some point, offered a pleasant but forced smile to a stranger, or maintained a face of deep concentration in class for the teacher's sake, even though we didn't study at all. Well, that is pure acting.

The objective of an actor's performance is to tap into the truth of a moment. As the actor-author of this book, I am about to tap into the very intense and honest truth of the craft. Ready? Here it comes: You really don't need to go to an acting class. An actor's job is to be human. If you are a human by any stretch of the word, then you can act.

In fact, even non-humans can act. One evening, upon arrival at my home, my dog, Marty, showed me he was hungry. He began running to the kitchen, wagging his fluffy tail, wide-eyed, panting, spinning in circles, even standing on his hind legs as I opened the cupboard. Just as I was about to hook him up with a second dinner, my girlfriend hit me with a text:

I fed Marty btw :))

Give Marty the Oscar. What a performance he delivered! Too bad there weren't cameras rolling at the time. But even if there were, Marty wouldn't have cared; and there's a valuable lesson from Marty for us actor-type humans to smoke on.

Acting ain't rocket science. In fact, it's perhaps the farthest thing. I'd say it's one of the easiest jobs on the planet, especially when you factor in that actors are ridiculously overpaid and over appreciated. We humans are already wired with the goods to convey emotions, right out of the box. If you can be touched by a poem, a song, a film, a play; or ticked off in traffic when someone cuts you off; or full of despair after the loss of a loved one, congratulations, you're a human being. And you have a wider emotional range than my sneaky dog.

When you're with complete strangers or in a casting room, the most important skill you'll want to have kick in is comfortability. You've got to be comfortable. Comfortable with uncertain circumstances, comfortable in your own skin, and, most of all, comfortable in front of a camera. This comes easier to some more than others, but in time you will master it. Some actors and performers are far more cozy before a camera than in a real social setting. Acting is their refuge. Luckily, I'm good either way.

As promised in the marketing of this book, I am not going to tell you how to act. I want to get you working in front of a camera, not delving into your past emotions, subconscious, or in your wallet, for that matter. I don't subscribe to any method or technique, be it Stanislavski or Stella Adler. If your aim is to kick it old school like that, I respect that, absorb these words and pass the book on to fellow acting friend. I am far from an authority on the acting craft. For that I would direct you to David Mamet's *True and False, Heresy for the Common Sense Actor*. That is a must-read for any actor looking to get crafty with it.

But I do possess my own kind of approach. Before a role, be it an infomercial or an indie film, I carry out two rituals. First, I ask myself who I see in this part beside myself. I flip through my mental Rolodex of famous character actors to hypothetically cast this very part that I am about to play.

For instance, consider the role of a disgruntled dad I just did in a horror short. Before going on set, I marinate in the possibilities of character-types, heroes, anti-heroes. That day, my mind cast a young Gene Hackman for this part. I then envisioned how he would bring the role to life. By the time the director yells action, I am Gene in my mind.

Mind you, I would not do an impression of the actor, but more so an interpretation. After all, I have zero resemblance to Gene Hackman. In addition to my hypo-casting approach, I remind myself that I am there to do a job, pure and simple. My objective is to deliver an optimum performance for the client, as well as showcase my services. This shows a good acting work ethic. And that leads to a good reputation. A good reputation leads to referrals, great footage reel and prominence on social media outlets.

When I was first entering the world of acting, I had a beginner's attitude. That is, arrogance. I was too cool for school. I thought, *How hard can this be whole acting thing be?* My unfounded hubris initially paid off as I actually started to book jobs.

I was soon at a point where I was actually turning down work; I was booked that much. I kept hitting my shots so much, I couldn't believe it.

Insert GIF of Michael Jordan's
famous shrug here.

As I began to catch my stride, I flirted with the idea of actually taking classes and turning down work to strengthen my craft. Classes, I thought, would only make me that much sharper out there in the world. My agent wholeheartedly agreed and encouraged me to sign up for instruction with a talented teacher locally whom I admire greatly—Stewart Solomon.

Stewart, bald-headed and full of brashness, could be any-where from 49 to 62 years of age. He's a buff guy and proud of it, which may be why he's always rocking tank-tops. Hailing from the New York theatre scene, where the real actors play, he tutors us unseasoned South Floridians with a hint of arrogance, as chances are most of us never have—nor ever will—step foot on a stage in the 212 area code.

There's no shortage of New Yorkers in Miami, earning it the affectionate nickname of *The Sixth Borough*. If only we had an efficient transit system in The 305, but that's not the case. So every Wednesday night, for six weeks, I endured the slow snake of I-95 rush hour brake lights en route to Aventura to join about 6 other students in Stewart Solomon's Creative Workshop.

The workshop took place in "the studio", which was the converted garage of Stewart's townhome. A little off-putting at first as I initially wondered if this guy and his operation were even legit. But, he already had my money, so there was no turning back. Plus it was still rush hour.

Meeting actors in an acting class is an accelerated way really get to know someone. Even if your shy, you'll soon be performing, baring your soul to the class, or at least trying to. Even if your skills are sub-par at first, a good teacher can brew a good performance out of you. Stewart assigned us each a monologue to study, make our own, and eventually perform for the class for each session.

We were quite the gaggle of characters, including the Ukrainian repairman whose introduction included the news that his wife had just left him and with his newfound freedom he was excited to explore his acting talents. During class recess, he would vent about his evil ex-wife while sucking back menthols. Apparently, she got the house, but he boasted that he got his life back. Moreover, he said, he got back his balls. He was using the class as a kind of therapy, a time for him to release his frustrations. I thought it a great idea—and a whole lot more cost-effective than actual therapy. During his monologue, no matter how many times Stewart instructed him otherwise, he insisted on shouting his lines, believing this made his performances more compelling. Imagine a one-note Al Pacino with a Russian accent.

Also, among our troop was a budding Instagram star, Julia. At that point she was just a VIP bottle girl at LIV, a premier nightclub on Miami Beach. She actually didn't stick out the six-week course, but in the two classes she did manage to attend, she stole the show. You could attribute her success to the fact that she was easy on the eyes, or that her adorable face effortlessly sashayed from emotion to emotion. Or maybe I am misremembering; perhaps it just might have been her physique that drew our attention and made everything else seem real. Even Stewart, who's gay by the way, was transfixed by her every move.

She was a beauty with spunk, a feast for the eyes and the soul. She was easy on the ears too, as she spoke with a fine-tuned Western Floridian voice, pitched with a hint of rasp only furthering her charm. I actually just Googled her, and the lady is certainly killing it as an influencer. When it comes to Julia, the theatre's loss is social media's gain. Damn you Instagram!

During our performances Stewart's passion for acting was very apparent. He would watch us intently, while sipping from an ever-present jug of water, and "channel the Acting Gods," as he put it, as he offered advice and feedback. His offerings were less interruptions and more ruminations, little bread crumbs of guidance to inspire us as we proceeded through our monologues. It was almost as if he would play us like instruments. If we needed some real fine-tuning and something just wasn't right, the Acting Gods would demand, through Stewart of course, for us to stop. At this point, the coach would ask: What is this scene about? One night, I was performing my assigned monologue. It was about a guy pleading to his wife that she is just too damn perfect. She's always making a great dinner, the sex is great, she never nags, etc. Stewart stopped me dead in my tracks and posed that age-old question: What is this scene about?

I answered that the guy is trying break up the routine of his perfect life. But Stewart cut me off again, turned to the Acting Gods and pleaded to know why his students were so naïve. Then he turned back and explained that the scene is about one thing only: "Pusssyyyyyyyyy," he said, drawing the word out to a hilarious yet embarrassing (for me) effect. He stressed that the majority of the scenes written in world theatre are about that dynamic. The sooner I saw that, he explained, the better my performances will be.

I was initially shocked. But the more I think about it, the more I break down life, the more I came to realize that Stewart was is right. Pussy, be it exactly that or some other alluring enticement, is the goal of most situations in life, especially in Miami.

After six weeks of fine-tuning my monologue, I also enjoyed the camaraderie that developed among the classmates. All raw talents all, we were vastly different from each other, but we connected as actors, as people who shared a common desire in cultivating their craft. Besides that, I was wholly entertained by the boisterous utterings of our leader. The experience was very enriching personally, I was growing as an actor, and the training was making me more marketable. Surely this was going to lead to more work. Right?

As I noted already, before the classes I was flying quite high and working constantly. Yet after the block of classes I fell into the worse slump of my acting career. Casting after casting, I was now missing my shots. What was it? My confidence hadn't gone anywhere. In fact it grew. I just spent six weeks under the tutelage of Stewart fucking Solomon and his pet Acting Gods. How could you not want me to star in your Tide commercial, Mrs. Casting Director? And therein lies the answer. I was too confident to the point where I may have been perceived as flippant. Stewart's teachings are too high brow for little commercial castings (usually). I soon realized I had to water down my performances for the commercial castings, but tap into the teachings of Stewart for the meatier roles.

Knowing when and how to dial it back is your job as an actor.

I recommend acting class to anyone, even non-actors, for the experiences of the people, but it will not automatically lead to more work and may even briefly have the adverse effect, as it did for me.

Also, look out for local casting directors that offer workshops. Chances are they exist. Some warn actors away from this, as they deem this as paying for auditions. But they are very effective for this very reason. They allow you to get an audience with the casting director. If they never knew you, now they do and can get a chance to observe you and your raw talent.

So you want to skip school altogether? School's not for everyone. No problem; just stay on your grind. Look out below as I drop a few names of actors that bypassed acting classes but ended up doing pretty okay for themselves: Tom Cruise, Johnny Depp, Meg Ryan, Russel Crowe, and Jennifer Lawrence.

WHO'S YOUR AGENT

"On your ascension for the stars,
your agent is air traffic control."
— Unknown

It's time to lift yourself out of the depths, rescue yourself from the trenches of underexposure. You know you're amazingly awesome, highly watchable and marketable. But not one casting director in town knows you even exist since you're unrepresented. You're the best-kept secret in town. You're all dressed up with nowhere to go. And that's a damned shame, since you got the goods, keen expressiveness, a wicked comedic timing, and the camera absolutely adores you. You could very well be the next Flo from the Progressive ads or that "Can you hear me now?" turncoat from the Verizon and Sprint commercials. You just might have the chutzpah to be bigger than a commercial actor. You could be the next action hero, the next Harrison Ford (impossible). All you need is an agent to get you there. An agent who will go to bat for you, send you to auditions, and get you paid. (And if she's really good, he will battle to get you higher rates.) An agent does all of these things, and if they're great they do much more.

Who's your agent? It's a question that actors ask each other after hello. It's a great way to start a conversation with a fellow actor. The questions that follow are typically: Do you like them? Do they pay on time? Did they get you any great jobs?

Regarding that last question, agents don't necessarily get you jobs. When it comes to auditioning, it's you who gets the job. It is you who got all dolled up and told the mirror you're dopest actor in the Western hemisphere. You're the one who attended the audition and had to pretend you're changing the diaper of a baby dinosaur (yes, I've had to do this). It is you who then meditated, asking the universe to please bestow the blessing of this deodorant commercial upon thee. Then, hooray, you were invited to the callback of that audition and did the baby dinosaur bit all over again. But this time the pompous director and clients were there as well, to offer their ideas as to how one would properly hold a baby triceratops.

You then hoped a little more and even prayed to the Gods who watch over all acting class. Days of painful silence occur.

Then your phone rings. It's your agent. You got the role of Dad! You then thank your agent, but they should be thanking you (which they do sometimes). Remember this: It was all you, all along. Your agent just told you when and where to go. You started merely as one of the horses in the race. But you ended up the triple-crown winner.

I didn't get my first agent until my 20's. Sure, this agent specialized in children, but it was still an exciting moment. To say the words "my agent" legitimized me. "My agent says this." "My agent just called."

Even though I had yet to get a job through her, I felt important. Eventually, I did manage to book my first real commercial—as the lead—through her. It was just a regional for some Chicago furniture store, but I was the man. The spot had me sitting on a bench with a lovely blonde, displaying a little PDA, much to the ire of a perfectly-casted, old lady on the other end of the bench. Just as I'm about to lay a kiss on my gal, the old lady rudely interrupts us and says, "Why don't you get a room!" That's how the furniture angle comes in.

Jockeying for an agent in a place like Florida is as simple as visiting their website. Some agencies have a submission portal right there on the site where you can upload your photos. Your new headshot should be enough. Along with your measurements, you'll want to include a personal note to the agent and a brief bio. Highlight what it is that drives you to be in this business and any relevant past experiences. As the case is in every space of human interaction, flattery goes a long way, especially if it's genuine. Research the agency, learn about its history and past projects of note. A submission letter could go something like this:

Dear (Agent)

Happy hump day to you! (If it's Wednesday) My name is Andy Guze and I'm an actor/model here in South Florida. I am currently seeking new TV and film representation, and I believe we are a great fit for each other. After studying at So and so's acting classes and attending big shot casting director's workshop, I truly believe that I am at a point in my career where I'm ready to book the kind of remarkable jobs that your team handles. I want to be a part of the roster of excellent talent at your (agency)!

Please review my attached headshot and resume. Follow the link to my reel and see clips of recent work. As you can see, I have a wide range of roles under my belt. Looking forward to meeting you and discussing working together. Thank you, (Agent name).

Best Regards

Andy Guze

Yes, that was a semi auto-biographical. If you can't yet offer reels or clips, read on; I will address that in a later chapter. Even if you have never been in anything ever, you can still have a reel.

The sunshine state of Florida is a right-to-work state. This means, among other things, as an actor you have no restrictions; you can work with as many agents as you damn well please. I currently work with three. I know some actors in Miami that have eight and other loyalists who stick with one.

A benefit of agency polygamy is that most agents have exclusive clients that they will only pull from their talent roster, and occasionally even directly book. A direct booking is the sweetest things for a working actor. It means you were directly booked in lieu of a hectic casting call. You've been blessed with the luxury of not having to jump through hoops and, instead, jumped right into a motherfucking job!

Another function of working with multiple agents is diversification. One agent may be your commercial agent, another may strictly be for print work, and another may focus on TV and film.

In Florida it is common for an agent to actually do it all, just like the actors down here.

Another reason for seeking the services of several agents is regional. You may live in Miami, but you want to market yourself in Orlando or Tampa or Atlanta. While obtaining a representative in different markets can be challenging, as agents prefer that you're a local, it can be done. It's easier to pull off in the smaller markets that are thirsty for talent. (NYC, LA, and now even Atlanta want you living in town in order to take you on.) I have heard of actors using other people's addresses to present themselves as a local, but those drives and flights are going to add up. Still, there's always that chance you could star in a new Amazon series or a beer commercial that goes viral.

Recently I did something unique to Miami; I got an agent strictly for Spanish speaking roles. At first glance, I know I don't exactly scream the Latin market, but I do speak Spanish pretty *bueno* and I do have Cuban roots. So after working on a short film where we shot each scene in both Spanish and English, I thought that I should monetize this secondary language skill. Telemundo, here I come.

I just needed the agent, and find her I did. We signed an agreement that she will be my exclusive agent for all things Spanish-speaking. She sent me to Telemundo Studios in Hialeah, FL, for my first telenovela audition. Bear in mind, I never actually watched a telenovela in its entirety, just snippets here and there while channel-surfing as kid. (Channel-surfing is a euphemism for another task involving my right hand and my teenage imagination, fueled by the sight of a telenovela beauty.) Now, in my mid-30's, I wanted to be part of the Spanish soap opera game.

At the auditions, only a few actors were called in at a time. The room where that actual read took place felt like an interrogation room. There was a cameraman and an acting coach. As I warmed up with my lines, the coach was already off put by my Spanish pronunciation. We read through the lines again, still no praise from the coach. My Spanish could fly for a short film, but Telemundo is the Spanish-speaking big leagues and you can't talk like a Gringo who drifts in an out of a Cuban accent. All telenovela actors are encouraged to learn to speak with a universal accent, which is Mexican. We eventually just barreled through a read and I was on my not so merry way. I knew I didn't get the role of Fulano. It was easy to rationalize the rejection. *Do you really want to be in a telenovela?* I asked myself. *You're way, way too cool for such a thing.*

Not only must an actor have thick skin, they must also have the talent of rationalizing the continual rejection endured over the years. So bad acting, bad lighting, bad story-line, hot women, telenovelas just weren't for me. I was fine, no I was happy with that. I preferred not being in telenovelas, what a blessing that I can't speak perfect Mexican Spanish. Wow, that was close! I could've been in a telenovela. I dodged a bullet of actor shame there. Then my Latin market agent called.

"Hola, Andy; they want to book you on a series." Say what? Wow. That's great! I was directly booked to play a recurring doctor on some other telenovela that I never even read for. I was shocked. They booked me for a role that I never read for and the only taste of me they have is my gringo appearance and my semi-broken Cuban Spanish. My agent then told me that the doctor character was actually going to be speaking in English. What a perfect fit. I know enough Español to be on a Spanish-speaking set, and my English is superb. The network was introducing more English-speaking characters to widen their audience.

My Telemundo streak began. First as an English-speaking recurring doctor. What a moment – I can now truly say that I'm not a doctor, but I played on TV. That was followed by a guest spot on a Christmas special, *Milagros De Navidad*, a heartwarming special. During the opening credits they established the show was taking place in Chicago. But then they open with me driving down a suburban Miami street lined with palm trees. Really?

Sometimes, actually usually, the production quality of these novela factories is subpar. I can't help but assume the minds behind the scenes know better, but they just barrel through it. They have more to do. Time is money. One hour of Telemundo TV costs only $70,000 to produce. So the result is quick takes, bad performances, weird lighting, and implausible locations. But just make sure you hit those Latino airwaves. Just a few factual glitches aren't enough to deter a devout viewership that spans generations and lives in over ten countries.

Then I got the biggest role of my life thus far: Johnny, a rowdy redneck with soft spot for hard drugs and xenophobia. He was the abusive ex-boyfriend of one of main stars. Again, this was another direct booking. The real beauty of playing Johnny was that I could rewrite my own lines because most of the people set didn't speak English. I made the Johnny character all mine, poured my heart into him. He ends up fleeing in his car with cops on his tail, crashes into a light pole. His strung-out ex-girlfriend bails, leaving poor Johnny unconscious in his car. He then wakes up to a group of cops with their guns drawn in his face. When Johnny helpfully reaches for his wallet to show ID, the cops kill him. What a way to go.

For those planning on venturing to LA-York with the hopes of getting represented by the Ari Gold's of the world, or the CAA, UTA, and Gersh agencies, fair warning: It's going to be a challenge. You can't just sign up. Their websites explicitly state: no unsolicited submissions. You could be the next Charlie Chaplin, but they will remain deaf and blind to you unless a trusted source has made the referral.

So what comes first, the chicken or the egg? The answer is, 9 times out of 10, the hot actor managed to land a big role with a

On location in a trailer park as "Johnny" in Mi Familia Perfecta / Telemundo 2018

second tier agency first. That caught the eye of the bigger agency that offered to represent him. That's just the nature of the business. You learn to bypass the gatekeepers of productions with your talents before the gatekeepers at the agencies will allow you to join their roster.

AUDITIONS

"The only failure is not to try."
— George Clooney

My very first audition experience dates back to the ebullient era of the 90's. The boy band craze was at its apex. Remember the faces of these posses of pop? They were everywhere – from magazine covers to bedcovers. All smiles. All awesome. All cheese. It was hard to look away. As a kid raised on rap, and a man who to this day marinates in the juices of good hip-hop, I am embarrassed to recollect that I actually imagined a life as a member of one of those overly-produced assemblages of candy-coated testosterone.

I can't exactly sing nor do I have a flair for dance choreography, but that didn't stop my best friend and I from attending an open audition for the world's next best boy band.

The audition demanded dancing and then singing. If you impressed the judges with your dancing skills, you were allowed to sing. They broke us into groups. We had to catch on quick to the choreographer's steps to a new song by Destiny's Child. As a guy of Cuban descent, I can move to the beat, but among these post-pubescent trained kids I didn't stand a chance. I might as well have been rocking two left Kenneth Cole loafers.

Amid my own personal dance crisis, I looked over to my friend. He shared my grief. We agreed to abandon the situation and stepped outside. I believe "Fuck this shit" may have been our phrase of choice as we sparked up our cigs.

Looking back, the boy band casting call was more of a wake-up call. It alerted me that I was an inexperienced, untrained talent, rawer than a plate of liver. Those others at the audition were veteran show kids. I merely had delusions of unfounded grandeur. It was the first of many reminders that this world is full of people who want to be in front of a camera. Whether you want to be a musical artist or actor, you have to work hard to stand out.

It wasn't until a chunk of years later that I found myself auditioning again, this time as an actor for a commercial. They had me wear a Superman costume that must have been tried on by thirty dudes before me while I smiled and said some stupid line. I was new and nervous. I had yet to understand how to effectively stand out to the casting director. Guess whether I got the job.

Here's my take on casting versus auditions. Then we'll get into tips for knocking them dead, breaking legs, and taking names.

A Casting

One may associate that word with fishing, so here goes my maritime analogy. In a casting, it's not just one single rod being cast in the sea to lure a fish. Actually, the producers are casting a wide net to catch as many qualified fish as possible.

The role may not call for much. Perhaps they just want to see how you sound, move, and interact with other actors. A casting is generic, you're supposed to be a mold of a familiar American type: The aging hunk, the girl next door, the soccer mom, the group of ladies on the town, the successful couple at a resort, a corporate leader, a fitness lady. They want to match the brand they're selling with the targeted demographic(s) that will likely buy the product or service. They like to keep it generic and watered-down so that the majority of viewers will connect with their television commercial. Once you know your type, you'll do much better in the general casting process.

An Audition

This is the classic show business audition. This requires acting. And it's not just for TV or film parts. Some commercials call for a level of acting that requires you to bring the goods as it were. The actor has to prepare, prepare some more, perform, and wow the powers that be in order to get the part. Your skill set should be an extensive one; know your lines, and have a deep understanding of the script and role before stepping into that audition.

One can expect the casting/audition process to go like this. You arrive at the casting director's office and sign in, providing your name, contact info, agent and your age—which everyone lies about. Or some just put their age range i.e. 25–40. In the past, you were expected to bring a headshot or a comp card. Those days are thankfully history.

You take a seat among the others, many of whom bear a resemblance to you. Then you patiently wait. If there are sides (the screenplay of the scene), you review that. Many times, there aren't sides at all, so you sit and look at your phone. (You could chat up fellow actors, but casting directors prefer you don't.) More waiting. Then they'll call you in.

Expect to see the casting director and an assistant who may be manning the camera. If there weren't any sides, the casting director will give you a quick rundown as to what you'll be doing for the camera. This can be basic or downright bizarre. I can't tell how many times I have been told to act as if I'm enjoying a sunset on the beach. Or, as previously recounted, changing the diaper of a baby dinosaur. They provide props or co-performers if needed. Before it's showtime, they'll ask you to slate.

A slate is the first time some of these shot callers will make your acquaintance. It basically entails addressing the camera, saying who you are, and who's your agent. Then you'll show off both your left and right side profiles. How strong is your side-game? A slate done well is a great way to splash into the good graces of a decision-maker. If not, it can lead to doom. I've heard of cases where the slate failed to wow them, so they ended the audition.

So I'd say just keep it real vanilla, as in simple, natural, and slightly charming. You can adjust your enthusiasm to the role at hand. This is where acting decisions come into play. What is charming? How enthusiastic? You got this. Speak clearly with confidence. Look directly into the camera's iris as if you have some love for it, with the goal of the camera loving you right back. And that's just the slate!

Now you get into you performance. Depending on what the scene calls for, you'll exchange lines with someone behind the camera, another actor in front of the camera or, all alone. Whatever the case, you gotta come with your acting game on point. Whatever the heck that means. This is art, so it can be subjective. But there are constant factors that help you get the part.

Prepare for the role. **Know your lines** forward, backward, upside down, in a house, with a mouse. Interrupting the flow of your performance with a "Um, sorry" is such a bad look. Almost as bad as the judgmental look on the faces of your audience after a flub. Remember that the casting director truly loves actors – and good acting. That's precisely why they do what they do. So make sure you know the lines, of course, but also the characters and their backstory. The more knowledge you possess of the content at hand, the more calculated your creativity. Now you can make those bold acting choices that the keepers of the gates crave. Then they'll be happy to cast you.

If this is a commercial audition, chances are there are no sides, and the casting director will give some kind of scenario prior to the performance. They may say something like this:

"Ok, Andy. So you've been busting your ass for your family, because you love them. But you need some dad time. So you just got this new TV Set and cable service and it's your weekend escape. So you take a seat on the couch with a remote and start to channel-surf. You stop at one channel and Spider-Man is on the screen. But suddenly he comes swooping into your mancave, takes a seat next to you, and puts his feet up. But you're not even that shocked. It's this new TV that you're really impressed with. So about 20 seconds in, act as if Spider-Man has arrived. (They'll add him in post.) Give him a little nod or even greet him like a bruh. Got it?"

This is where improv skills serve you well. The more you get to know yourself, the more you'll have your variety of go-to reactions and facial expressions. Pretending to channel-surf and enjoying cable service is easy; but keeping one's cool around your friendly neighborhood Spider-Man, that's true talent.

After your performance, you thank the decision-makers and leave. Just a pleasant thank-you and peace the heck out of there. Leave them wanting more. You'll feel accomplished. You satisfied a very important task. Now you wait.

At first you may lose sleep over whether you got the job or not. Eventually you grow a thicker skin and realize, like I did, that it's no longer my concern, until my agent calls and says, "You're booked!" I no longer spend hours trying to guess how I did or how they liked me.

Trust me, I wasn't always so cool. For years it was quite frustrating, auditioning, and waiting, hoping every time the phone rang it was my agent with some good news. But, that will drive one crazy. Just let it be like the lads from Liverpool. Rejection is normal, almost a pillar of an actor's life.

You may have crushed your audition and are the clear choice for the part, but there are so many factors out of your control that determine who is hired. And some of the decisions are loony tunes. Imagine that you remind the client of her cheating ex-boyfriend. You're dead in the water—even if you were the best choice.

As the un-pushy Car Salesman for Lexus. Here's to crushing your audition and good sets with good coffee.

SETS AND LIFE

"You can make more friends in two months
by becoming interested in other people than
you can in two years by trying to get other
people interested in you."
— Dale Carnegie

Among the many delights of being an actor is being on a set. Actually, let me be specific: I mean a union-style set, a set of the grandiose variety. A set where the professionalism is tip-top. It's where actors have their own trailers and even the assistants have assistants. A meticulous set where the crew are walking hardware stores, cleverly solving any emergency. Another sign of the real set: Craft services is a smorgasbord of both healthy delicacies and tempting junk food that looks like the dressing room offerings for an arena-level rock star.

Being on set is your chance to leave a lasting impression on some decision makers that can lead you to more work. How does one be memorable? A fellow known as Dale Carnegie wrote a book about *How to Win Friends and Influence People* back in the 1930's. It remains relevant to this day and can be implemented in all lines of work and life. Read it, twice. One tip Carnegie provides is about the power of compliments.

The University of Miami football team has taken it one step further. They've adopted a tradition known as the turnover chain. When the Miami defense is on the field and happens to get a turnover, be it by fumble or interception, he who made the play is then rewarded with a turnover chain. It's a chunky gold necklace with the Miami logo dangling off it. It's a token appreciation. This idea can be used on sets to make friends among fellow actors and the crew.

Hit the set with your own metaphorical version of the turnover chain. Find something praiseworthy about the people you encounter and let it be known. The director of photography beautifully lit the scene? Give him your thanks. Lunch was delectable? Let catering know your taste buds are thoroughly satisfied. Is the writer on set? Hit them with a hearty compliment. If you find it pleasing, interesting, or impressive, let people on set know. Emanate positivity. And watch how quickly the vibe changes for the better.

Pardon me as I interrupt this chapter with a little poem I dreamt up while on a set a few years back in Tampa, FL.

ODE TO THE CREW

Day breaks and day rates
Crew call of duty
Pepper cheese and egg whites
And maybe a smoothie
Production guys
Get it done with pride
I'm talking film and TV
Or spot commercialized
It's all about the frame

And what pops within
Behind the scenes Steady Teems
with hard working men... And women
C-stands and plans
Gripping tools with hands
Holding down the set-up
Like bags of sand - firm
Make it bounce and turn
Contemplating illuminating
Watch that DP earn that loot
Rightfully so
Lens speed scene captured
Magically so
So many factors before actors
Make believe as they do
If you love the screen
You better love the crew

....and we're back

Of course targeting the above-the-line folks is shrewd for the actor. It's a way of planting the seeds for in the future. I always make it a point on set to introduce myself to the producers, thank them for having me, and offer praise of the project. This also goes for the director—even if you feel they were abrasive or difficult to satisfy. It's an unfortunate but common dynamic—and it happened to me on a huge commercial shoot where I was the lead.

This was one of those a top-shelf union shoots. As the hero, I had a wardrobe fitting prior to the shoot date, which was also a stunt rehearsal. Yes, a stunt rehearsal. They had your boy in a harness attached to a pulley system that was to be yanked as my actress wife had set booby traps to prevent me from touching the thermostat. We've all been there, right?

This was just a one-day shoot and at the helm was a reputable director who was overtly particular about what he wanted. Which I actually like. When a director is hellbent on their vision being realized, I am more than happy to oblige them, unless I am at a loss as to how to make that happen. The first shot of the commercial is me walking into my home. I already suspect that my wife will have set traps and obstacles of green laser beams to deter me from getting to the thermostat. I got the job because of a sly reaction shot to the wife's schemes.

The crew and I were ready to roll and take one. But the director shouts cut and calls me aside. He reminds me to flash the exact expression that I did at the casting. Easy enough. Surely I can muster up that exact expression. But as take after take was shot, the director was growing more frustrated. I could feel the pressure mounting as he yelled cut after every failed expression. I heard sighs from the grips and the clients were starting to panic. Take 5, take 6—and the director was now shouting at me in his thick Spaniard accent.

He called me to the outside hallway so we were alone. He looked at me with pleading eyes, asking, "What do I have to do to get this expression out of you?" I insisted that I was flashing the same expression that nailed the audition. But I wasn't. At this point I knew it was all me. I was being unsettled by the set.

I told the director I guess I just felt more comfortable in the casting room, where there was fewer people around. He seemed to understand and suddenly screamed that the set had to be cleared, save for all crucial people. In this case, just me and the director and the camera operator.

I was just full of jitters. There I was, literally living out a dream, to be leading man on big shoot, even if it was a Mitsubishi Electric commercial, and I was stuck.

He called action, I walked into the scene, hit my mark, and easily nailed the look that got me booked. We then kept it moving without a hitch and had the AD re-open the set. I respected that director and was happy I was able to deliver. But even if you can't, remember it's just a gig. This, too, will soon pass.

On the set of the Mitsubishi commercial nervous as hell before the director's pep talk and closure of the set.

EXTRA FLY

"I gotta testify, I come up in the
spot looking extra fly."
— Kanye West

Extra work is rock-bottom, entry-level acting. Imagine you're looking at a totem pole. Each totem represents the hierarchy of the personnel on a film production. So, the extra is on the very bottom, that part that is jammed into the earth and partially hidden. Extras don't even receive credit, nor have access to craft services. A PA may be sent to whatever area has been aptly designated as "extra holding" to drop off a little bag of chips, pretzels, and bottles of generic water. Extras lose their identities on set; they are referred to as "background." They are wrangled to and from set—like cattle.

But the clever and/or fortunate ones do not remain extras all their lives. There are plenty of actors of stratospheric success that were once suffocating in obscurity. Names like Ford, Pitt, and Travolta were all once extras. So as Indiana Jones, Tyler Durden, or Vincent Vega would, take those extra gigs in stride. And don't get too discouraged with respect to extra work, as some extra gigs are cushy, memorable, and fun.

At this point in my career, I won't do extra work. But I've sure had my fair share of extra experiences. Aside from several extra horror stories that come to mind, there is an extra's dream-come-true that I enjoyed. This was actually one of my first gigs ever as an actor and it was on a true-blue Hollywood set. And I'm not talking Hollywood, FL. The movie is called *Confessions of a Shopaholic*, starring Isla Fisher. If you're drawing a blank, she's the cute-as-a-button, yet psychotic, redhead from the smash hit comedy *Wedding Crashers*. The one who crazily tried to seduce Vince Vaughn. She's also Borat's wife. (That must be one hilarious household.)

The folks from production instructed me to bring a suit to the Ice Palace Studios. There they had constructed a set to look like an elevator and office building hallway. We were about six extras in total. This was quite the departure from previous extra gigs I had, where I had been working among 100 plus and kept outside in a tent. This scenario was very posh.

One of extras was actually a club door guy on South Beach. I recognized him immediately flashing back to many nights of being denied at the entrance unless I had a pack of girls or was willing to drop a couple grand on table service. Yeah, I kinda hated him at first, but we bonded on set and nowadays, he drops the velvet ropes if I happen to be out and about and see him poised in front of a club. Our task as extras was to just stand in the elevator as Isla Fisher, the star, scurried on, trying to evade an antagonistic bill collector. The extras and I stood in the elevator, some deboarding, others getting on while the scene played out. We must've done several takes, with the assistant director guiding us extras and the director directing the two actors. That is until the Acting Gods intervened. They possessed the director and urged him, with his suave English accent, to ask my name.

There I was, some new-jack extra in a suit, and the director wanted to know my name. Cue the angelic choir. I replied. "Andy," he continued, "the next time Isla gets on the elevator, say good morning."

Whoa!

I had to squelch my excitement and allow the actor to take over. Pretend this is just any other morning in an office building, you're an office guy named Andy, but you get to say "Good morning" to Hollywood starlets. After a solid half-day's work, I filled out my new union paperwork as an actual day player and left the set on a cloud—the ninth, to be exact. Within a few weeks, I received my first union check of my life, and a few months after that I received an invitation to the premiere of the movie. Glorious.

This is the big time, I thought. I booked a flight to Cali, fetched a date, and rolled up to the premiere looking extra fly. But there was no signature red carpet. Huh? I soon learned this was the second-tier premiere for the common folk. OK, whatever. All good.

Popcorn and soda in hand, my date and I found some seats as the house lights dimmed. Never having read the script, I wasn't quite sure as to when I'd grace the screen. Turns out it was toward the end of the first act. There I fucking was, on the big screen. I leaned over and whispered to my date "Here comes my line."

Guess what? They cut it. I sunk down in my seat, and later fled the theater with my date to sink a few stiff drinks. Hey, it's ok.

I'm still standing, right there, in the elevator next to the leading lady. But rejection is real.

Being an extra just may be the easiest job to get on a production. Easier than being a PA, an assistant, or even an intern. And now marinate in this for a hot second: an extra is essentially the same occupation of say Julia Roberts, or any actor for that matter. An extra's job is to make believe—just as it is for any bit part, cameo, supporting actor, or lead. While an extra is making believe in a smaller capacity—pretending to walk from work, enjoying a drink, sharing a conversation—they are making believe nonetheless. They are still making believer while the camera pushes past them to feature those higher on the credits. To be an extra may be easy, but it's blatantly by far the most challenging to be extra-successful at.

Intermingling on sets among the crew, cast, and the different departments is a given. The production business is a small world, people tend to know each other, and inevitably develop bonds and friendships over the years from set to set. This too occurs among the extras. And from my experiences, in front and behind the camera, the extras bond harder than them all. They're complete strangers at call time, typically in the wee hours of the morning, representing all walks of life, backgrounds, and cultures, unified by their current reality of being at the bottom and their audacious hopes of one day getting out of the trenches. Extra holding can feel akin to high school detention, the bonding is inevitable and accelerated, and by the last shot of the day, they just may be life-long friends, like the Breakfast Club. Don't you forget about me.

As mentioned, I still consider extra work from time to time. My interest perks up when it's a SAG gig as I know I'll be treated with dignity and decently paid in a timely manner. Currently, for 8 hours of extra-ing, the SAG scale for commercial background is $342.40. Not bad. That's pretty much a plane ticket anywhere within the continental US, a slick new pair of head-turning kicks, or a modest down payment on a pair of red-bottom stilettos (ladies?). Another exception to considering extra work is the adventure factor, IE: travel. A few years back I was presented with the opportunity of a print extra job. The pay was ok, but the real draw was shooting down in Puerto Vallarta, Mexico. Wait; they'll willing to pay me to go on a vacation to the Mexican Riviera? Sign me up. Sure, your boy would be at the mercy of the production and may have an awkward schedule, but after Googling the resort where we were to be staying, I saw the swankiness was next-level. The job was a cakewalk, including the bonus of an all-inclusive vacation with free booze. The only catch was early call times – but that meant early wrap times. Otherwise, I just had to hang around set to be available to lend my out-of-focus likeness for the camera which was focused on the more beautiful leads with killer bods and radiant smiles. A week after some much needed R & R, I was back in Miami, rejuvenated. Two weeks after that, I was compensated for background services, even if they were out of focus. Not bad at all.

I fondly recall another extra gig with a similar promise of a being-paid-to-vacay scenario. This time it was on the high seas, aboard an obscenely colossal Royal Caribbean vessel. It was for some sappy Hallmark movie starring the now-grown-up girl from

Spy Kids and her husband whom I knew from my MTV casting days. For a week, I was part of a squad of pumped-up extras cruising the Caribbean. It felt less like a job and more like an adult summer camp and the cool veteran PA was more like our cool camp counselor.

Once I knew I was to be booked on this vessel, I decided to produce a rap song called "Cruizn'" prior to the voyage. I shot the video on board, enlisting fellow extras as the co-stars and iPhone camera operators. For extra, extra credit, go to YouTube and watch: Cruizin by Azim Rock.

KEEP IT REEL

"I've never made any film that I
wouldn't go back and edit."
— Michael Mann

Let's talk about compiling your show business reel. First, allow me to draw some parallels. A movie is a collection of clips that are pertinent to the overall story. If what we are watching does not move the story forward, it's a waste of time, celluloid, and talent. (Although that does keep me from asking myself, when does Chewbacca go to the bathroom in *Star Wars* or who's feeding the army of the Unsullied at the battle of King's Landing in *Game of Thrones*.)

While potentially fascinating, these are still just irrelevancies that don't serve the story. So they needn't be addressed. Such is also the case in an actor's reel, a collection of clips meant to you showcase your staggering talent.

When cutting this video version of a business card, remember that this is about you. Sure, you share scenes with other people. But this is a greatest hits of your look, your voice, your range, your type, and your experience. So make sure you mostly show you and only you.

A headshot is a flat, unmoving snapshot of you. Reels bring that headshot to life before our very eyes and show you in the middle of work as an actor. Reels allow casting directors, agents, and producers to get an idea of how you move, sound, Does the movie camera love you? How does the light paint your face? How does your voice convey feeling through the dialogue? Reels offer validity to an actor and his career, even in the minor roles. Oh, you played Cop 2 on *Burn Notice* season 3? I see you. You were that guy from that Lexus commercial that kept popping up during my YouTube watching? Cool beans.

Back when I was starting out, I had just finished my third job and I knew it was time to make my first reel. It may have been a bit premature, but I was jonesing to make my mark. The reel consisted of a Boston Market commercial, where I was happily mauling a piece of chicken; a bizarre medical show called *The Knee Diaries*, (don't ask); and my famous, scene-stealing "Good Morning" line that was cut from the comedy *Confessions of a Shopaholic*.

As proud I was of my first reel, it didn't really ace it. You know how I have talked about knowing which type you are, and focusing on that type in promoting yourself as an actor? Well, I didn't know the rules back then, so naturally I broke the rule. My reel was, in hindsight, a confusing compilation of clips where I was all over the place character-wise. It wasn't really me—or rather, the me that I wanted to be in the acting community.

However, I didn't realize the schizophrenic vibe of my reel back then. Hell, I was just happy to have gathered together all the footage. It wasn't easy. Getting the footage of the work was a mission. It remains that way. I've had to kick into nagging mode at times—and you know how shy I am—continuously emailing producers from past projects for access to the work. My gathering efforts have occasionally been in vain when I realize belatedly that the projects failed to see the light of day. Such as this little pilot where I was fortunate enough land a leading role. It was a period piece about the life of John DeLorean.

Since I was born in the 80's, and since I am a card-carrying nostalgia junky, I was stoked to be on board. I even did it for low pay. This was one of those exceptional cases where the love factor outweighed the business factor. Besides, it was only a three-day shoot.

It was all a cool time warp for me during that shoot, from the stone washed jeans to the vintage New York Seltzer bottled soda my character was sipping. I spoke in an 80's dialect, dropping words like "bitchin'" and "chill pill".

After numerous calls and emails to the producer about the film, I had to come to terms with the creeping realization that the producer wasn't releasing anything to the world. Perhaps after the denial of syndication from the networks, his ego was crushed, his heart was broken, and he had turned his back on the business. It was still good work and an accomplishment nonetheless. In the end, I never got the footage and all I had to show for the shoot was $550.00 (And some great memories.) It happens. More than one might expect. How does an actor cope? Sometimes you just have to take a pill of the chillest variety and move on to the next project. Keep in mind that no project is wasted time, even if it was never seen. You still came away with your acting chops sharpened, and there's nothing wasted about that.

I am a big proponent of reels. When they are compiled properly, they can get you either an agent or directly booked as a result. A headshot can't really do that.

I encourage new actors to get a superb reel as soon as possible. But, you ask, how can I have a reel without having done any work? Well, as I mentioned a few chapters back, you can always work for free on student projects. Or you can produce your own reel. Yes, slap on a producer hat and make a reel.

Select up to four scenes, offering a range of characters, that will best showcase your services. Include your strengths and your quirks. Perhaps you're Southern accent is as pretty as a peach or you have a knack for pretending to be heartbroken, hopeless sap who has seemingly lost it all. Hire a competent shooter who can light and capture audio. Find a shooter who has directorial aspirations that can also offer guidance. It will require some pre-production, writing, wardrobe, locations. But don't worry about casting—you got the part!

If you don't have production nerd friends, there are services for hire. They will produce your clips professionally, from the script to the scene to the post. They'll see it all the way through. It'll cost ya some serious bread, but once you book that national bread commercial, you'll recoup your investment—and then some. Be aware that these services may only be available in NY or LA, from my current research. But that could change by the time you read this.

Whether you're actually producing a reel from scratch or stitching together a collection of clips, your reel should be all about the many shades of you. Avoid including lines from other characters unless your brief interaction really shows you off to your best ability. In fact, avoid including any footage that is not immediately about you, you, you! Your reel should primarily showcase you and your acting talents—not your co-stars. Put your best foot forward and get reel!

WORK 2 WORK

"Hustle beats talent when talent doesn't hustle."
— Ross Simmonds

In the world of *showbiz* and baseball, you're only as good as your last hit. You landed a great role in an indie film that found streaming distribution on a renowned platform. That's great, they'll say. But that was two months ago. The casting director may go all Janet Jackson on your ass and ask, "What have you done for me lately?" Ouch. But it's a fair question—and one you need to be continually asking yourself. Better yet, stop asking yourself and start getting answers. It may mean rearranging your priorities. You'll need to spend less time stalking your ex (unless your ex is, say, top-tier director Kathryn Bigelow) and more time stalking the points of contacts that could lead to more work. The two fronts that will be requiring a hustler's spirit are your organic network and your future network.

ORGANIC NETWORK

These are the fine folks you meet in your journey through every-day life. Like that woman you met at Whole Foods while reaching for overpriced organic produce (just kidding; no, not really). Real talk, these are those basic everyday connections you have collected along the way, whether it be on a job at a party or on line at Space

Mountain.

Amass a contact list of emails, numbers, and social media links. Keep them updated on the progress of your career. New headshot featuring your spotty beard? Announce that to your network. New reel? An award perhaps? Blast that news out as if you were your own personal PR agency, for no other soul will do this for you. And just as you're hoping for your campaigns to garner positive results, show support for your members of your network. Inquire about their work, share their projects to your social, praise them on their accomplishments. Your network is nothing unless you're keeping in touch and keeping it fresh with daily updates.

FUTURE NETWORK

Your potential network. The industry players (and wannabe playaz) that you can keep engaged only if you submit, submit, submit. To build your future network, you'll have to scour on-line job postings on a daily basis, preferably twice a day. Some websites even have alerts that notify when casting for your type is posted. So make sure to set these alerts and act fast.

What are those websites, you ask? Here's a few:
+ Casting Networks
+ Backstage
+ Actors Access
+ Mandy

In concert with your efforts to find jobs and build your future network, your agent should be getting you into auditions. As I mentioned in the chapter on jobs, auditions are typically on the shortest of notice. Off to ride your new bike or meet an old friend for coffee? Think again, actor. You have an audition.

In fact, there could be an entire day's spent hopping around from casting to casting. Barrel through it, keep your spirit high, and show up. It is on days like this that your car will also serve as your portable wardrobe department. Taking on and off pants in a car may drum up some high school memories or have you second-guessing your career choices. But see it through. Once you book that job, it will all make perfect sense.

Of course, an actor needs to stay in perpetual motion. You did your thing, exceeding the director's expectations, and hit your marks. You shared it on The Gram. You reveled in the praise, the likes, the love, the fire, and clapping hands emojis. And then dust settles. So what's your next move? Sitting on your laurels isn't an option. Because even the best high-profile job will come and go. Have you been hustling in the meantime? Have you been allocating your efforts to your Organic and Future Networks? If so, hopefully you're on to the next one. If not, what are you waiting for, bruh? An engraved invitation? Unless you're Tom Cruise or Jennifer Lawrence, that invite just ain't gonna come. You're going to have to run after it.

There are instances in my life, to be honest, when I was guilty of actor's laziness. Does it sound more dignified if I call it complacency? Either way, it's a professional pitfall. But it's also understandable. After a big job, you always think you're now hotter than a tamale and people are going to call you because they desperately want a piece of that *fuego*. This mindset is delusional. It usually combined with a major case of hope. Let's call the actor in this mindset a hope dope.

The hope dope is living on hope. You hope the phone will ring. You hope a juicy new email will announce a new job offer. You hope. You hope. You hope when you're off to sleep. You hope when you rise. Not a good look. Fuck hope. Say no to hope and get pro-active. Stay on your grind and start generating sweat equity again. Act like the hungry first-time actor that you used to be, energetically going out on auditions and following up on every opportunity. Soon enough, Acting Gods permitting, producers will be taking notice again.

Sure, this acting game is a merciless ego bruiser; after all, weren't you just on top of the world in your last job? But that's how it goes. You're always climbing back up that mountain – or scaling the Hollywood Hills, if you prefer.

I'm reminded of a difficult but typical situation which eventually yielded me some sweet results. There was an audition for a feature film. I attended. I read. My agent reported that they liked me and wanted to put me on hold. Sure, agent. You got it. I'm on hold.. even though being on hold is an actor's purgatory. Because it means giving up other possible jobs.

I held those dates. I held on dearly. Those dates, I told myself, were the dates I was going to be in a movie. Positive thinking is crucial in these sit-and-wait cases. I had just finished watching *The Secret*, so I convinced myself this role was pretty much in the bag. All I had to do was envision myself, like the film instructed, getting the job and magically I would get it.

The dates got closer and closer, and my negativity began to creep back into my soul. My agent said she hadn't heard a thing. This kind of stuff happens, she said sympathetically. Now, that's true; a production gets a little ahead of itself and begins casting before the finances are locked in.

Whatever the situation, the dates I was vehemently holding came and went. And I never heard a thing. Totally ghosted. Then, a year or so later, I found myself wondering again about the role that never was. Perhaps masochistically, I excavated the old email about the holding of the dates. There I saw that the producer's email was CC'd on the message.

What the hell, I thought. I sent an email his way inquiring about the project. And within a day I had a response. A friendly response. Pre-production, the producer informed me, was back into full swing and the timing of my follow-up could not have been more clutch.

They invited me in to read again, this time for a supporting role. And damn, I landed that role. It was a little romantic comedy called *Make Love Great Again*. It did well on the festival circuit and eventually was picked up by HBO, streamable on all their platforms. moral of the story? Don't be afraid to be on top of matters. Sure, I'm probably the best actor in Miami. Sure, I totally brought the goods to the casting room that day. But the naked truth is that I got that role because I followed up.

Bringing this chapter home, I'll leave you with this final thought. An actor's job is about exposure. Exposure leads to jobs. When it comes to castings and audition requests, you go. Always. There are two casting directors in my fair city who are at the top of the game when it comes to scripted productions for TV and film. I've been sent to their auditions for ten years-plus now. But get this: I have yet to book one single job through them. None, nada, zero, zilch. That's ten plus years of rejection. It can wither one's spirit, but I still go regardless. One, because they keep requesting me so they must find me somewhat appealing. Two, it's a good acting exercise. And three, it's in my job description. And despite the failed attempts to land a role through these Miami casting titans, I've still managed to get on many cool scripted projects. Why? because I fulfilled the self-promotional duties of my job description. And you should, too. Once again, cultivate your networks.

MONEY

"When it comes to art, money is an
unimportant detail. It just happens to
be a huge unimportant detail."
— Iggy Pop

As an actor at the auspicious start of your hustle, the work is far more important than the money. Working for free is almost a given as a newbie to the game.

The experience you occur is invaluable to your skillset, confidence, and clout. The work is what leads to a career.

One of the classic forms of compensation a newbie may encounter from directors and producers may go a little something like this:

You will get credit in the film, two square meals. Then they may sweeten the pot with the promise of working with a great crew of creatives (OMG, really?) and potential additional exposure since they will submit the film to festivals.

Yep, there's a reason why they call this part of your acting career the hungry years. But it's not the 1930's and The Great Depression isn't in full swing, so two square meals ain't gonna cut it. Still, this is what's called paying your dues. Go for every job you can, even if they're not offering money.

The phase of free work brings you one step closer to your dream, from a wanna-be mindset to a gonna-be mindset. The moment you accept a role, even if there's no money, you now have the bragging rights of calling yourself an actor. Even if the occupation isn't money in the bank just yet, you're banking performances, experiences, connections, techniques, and fodder for a reel. And that's experience you can't buy.

Sometimes a fellow artist is trying to bring an idea to life, but he's unable to cough up some cash for your services. It's a familiar scenario which I am sympathetic to. A film crew of people donating their sweet time and faith is inspiring, whether the result is a success or a disaster. And actors helping actors up the ladder is never a bad thing.

Stay open to rare opportunities. But don't get a reputation for being easy. You shouldn't be free for just anything. Be sensitive to someone trying to exploit your mug for a commercial or marketing piece. That's where I draw a line. Even if you're just starting out, this is plain uncool. Actors, new or seasoned, should never have to act in commercials without earning a check. Imagine asking the guys hanging billboards to roll one up for free, out of the kindness of their heart.

I have done plenty of free gigs in my younger days as an actor. There is one that is locked to my memory like Super Glue, no matter how hard I try to shake it. There's this film festival down in Miami called The 48 Hour Film Fest. It's all in the name. Each film submitted must have been written, shot, and cut all within the span of 48 hours. I believe I saw the ad on Craigslist. It read: Seeking Actors For Project Shooting Tonight. The ad made it clear that there was no money involved, but also made it clear that there would be cool crew of filmmakers, and—the clincher—pizza.

I submitted my resume—which included a lot of white space at the time—and my headshot through email. The director called me within five minutes. He had a youthful Miami accent and asked if I was available that night for the shoot. He promised it wouldn't take more than two hours. That pizza was calling my name. Without hesitation I was in. In hindsight, I should have probably inquired as to what exactly the role called for. (Always ask).

I arrived at a Kendall, Florida, townhouse community that goes by the name of Lakes of the Meadow. I was instantly greeted with a not-so-cold beer. This was more of a get-together party setting than a no-budget film set. The director introduced me around to the baby-faced crew. I was no more than five years their senior, but I still felt old and out of place. I met the young gal who was playing my girlfriend. She resembled a *Fast Times Phoebe Cates*, just a tad more buxom, more Cuban.

OK, I thought, trying to see the bright side. Free beer, pizza, and a cute on-screen girlfriend. This doesn't suck at all.

They resumed shooting her scene where she was angrily packing a suitcase and making an exit or an escape. I didn't really know what to do with my downtime. (The beer was getting warmer.) Since I was a smoker at the time, I stepped onto the balcony to smoke and observe the shoot. She repeated the packing scene a couple of times, with the beer-drinking crew shouting out suggestions for retakes. Finally they got the shots, performances, and coverage they needed.

The director joined me out on the balcony and patted my back. "So Andy, are you cool with a little kissing scene?" Glancing at my on-screen girlfriend as she flipped her hair, I easily said "sure." But, then she then popped out to the balcony, gave a winning smile, and said "Bye."

What?

The director explained the scene ahead of me: My kiss would be shared with another guy. Say what? I hadn't seen the script, so the director explained: The reason my girlfriend character was packing her bag was because she discovered my character is in the closet. Oh.

Ok, I am as anti-homophobic as the next guy, but I just didn't think I should do it. I was broke back then and the idea of getting all *Brokeback Mountain* just seemed like a tall order for an inexperienced actor. Plus, as I mentioned, this was more of a house party with cameras than a serious film set. In other words, amateur hour.

I told the director that I'm sorry, but I'm not cool with kissing another dude. His disappointment was palpable among the crickets of a Miami summer night.

Just then the other actor arrived. The director pointed him out and explained to me that he was a cool guy—as if his coolness would make me more open to kissing him. I lit another cigarette and got very clear. I told the director that I won't be kissing that guy or any guy tonight or any night, but I wanted to help him tell his story, so we would find some creative alternative. We improvised with long embraces, Eskimo kisses, and spooning to replace the Hollywood gay kiss that never was.

It was still uncomfortable for me. I left the set that night feeling perturbed. I couldn't adhere to exactly what the script and the director called for. Did that make me a disingenuous actor? In retrospect, no; it just made me a person with limits and an actor, whether new or seasoned, who wasn't willing give his all to script that was hastily written with the ultimate goal of producing some little movie within 48 hours for a gimmicky film festival.

I soon learned to become an actor who asks what every performance entails. Now I make sure I can get a copy of the script beforehand, and know exactly what kind of production situation I will be entering.

Working for free is now in the rearview for me, as it should be. Still, I keep my business wits at the ready because people in this industry can often be more full of shit than money. Nowadays, when I am offered a job or even requested to audition or send in a tape, I ask three simple questions:

1. *What dates are you planning on shooting?*

Kind of important, No need to audition if I already know I'll be in Dallas, Epcot, or at a family wedding during that time. Of course, if it's a great project, better believe your boy will break some plans.

2. What is the rate?

Is this job even worth my time? Oh, so it's $250 for an exterior full-day and I got to drive to Broward County? Na, I'm good, bruh.

3. What exactly will I be doing and for how long? Will there only be video or will they be shooting stills as well?

Will I be wearing clown make-up on the beach in August? (Yep, had to do that.) Eating copious amount of chicken and spitting it out? No thanks. Oh, you're gonna fire off some stills? Yeah, that's another fee.

4. Usage. Where will this project be distributed? Online? TV? What regions? For how long?

These questions are key and if the producers can't answer any of these questions, they have some more pre-production to do before they start booking talent. This is one of the great functionalities of agents; they can filter out all the bullshit that abounds. But as I often acquire work on my own, you learn to act as your own agent and avoid unpleasant surprises.

If you manage to book some work on your own, always get payment that very day. This is why:

A few years ago I was booked on a magic car cleaner commercial. The producers contacted me via backstage.com. They said they needed my services for a half-day. All went well swimmingly on the shoot. I showed up, wielded the miracle product with amazement for the camera, shared some laughs with the crew, and I was wrapped. The producer assured me I would be getting my check within the next week.

That next week turned into that next month which turned into the month after that, which turned *me* into...The Nagging Man, an unmasked superhero, whose sole purpose was to get what was it rightfully owed to him for an honest day's work.

The Nagging Man stopped at nothing in the face of apathy and unresponsiveness, berating his employer with weekly emails, phone calls, and text messages. Although these attempts were futile, the Nagging Man even considered giving up. All was lost—until The Nagging Man searched inward for the strength to up the ante, to look into the eye of the tiger if you will. Our superhero located the company's street address in an email. So four months after the car cleaner shoot, the Nagging Man took a field trip out to Doral, FL, for truth, justice, and the American way.

EXT. OFFICE SUITES — DORAL FLORIDA — AFTERNOON

ANDY as THE NAGGING MAN, quickly pulls into a parking spot, exits His CAR. He looks up at the SIGN above the office suite. It reads: Shady Producer Productions.

The Nagging Man smirks, shakes his head, and walks to the office door. Determined.

INT. SHADY PRODUCER PRODUCTIONS — CONTINUOUS

A DING from the door sounds as The Nagging Man enters the office. He raises an eyebrow at the sight of SECRETARY, who has just put the final touches on her pedicure.

> SECRETARY
>
> Hey… Andy?

> NAGGING MAN
>
> The producer around?

> SECRETARY
>
> Um, yeah, but he stepped out for lunch.

> NAGGING MAN
>
> I'll wait.

The Nagging Man, cool as a fan, takes a seat. He notices the car cleaner PRODUCT that he was hamming it up with months prior. He flashes an artificial smile with Secretary as she admires her nails. Then:

In walks PRODUCER with a bag of LUNCH.

PRODUCER

They are out of platanitos. Can you
believe that?

From the look on the Secretary, Producer sens-
es something is amiss. He then turns to see The
Nagging Man .

PRODUCER

Andy.

NAGGING MAN

You have money for Pollo Tropical, but
You don't have money for your actors?

Producer deflects to Secretary.

PRODUCER

Didn't we send that out?

Secretary pretends to check, fumbling in some
papers then consulting her computer.

SECRETARY

Uhh… looks like we still have to
get that out to you, Andy.

The Nagging Man curiously looks to the
Producer.

> **PRODUCER**
>
> Ok. Well thanks for bringing this to
> our attention. We are on it.

> **NAGGING MAN**
>
> Oh, are you? On it. That's rich.

The Nagging Man calmly reaches for a PEANUT BUT-TER CUP from the CANDY BOWL, leans back, and unwraps the treat. He means business.

> **NAGGING MAN**
>
> But I'm not leaving until I
> get my money.

The Nagging Man pops the candy in his mouth and chews. Then reaches for a MAGAZINE. He flips through it.

Producer pauses then looks at Secretary.

EXT. OFFICE SUITES — DORAL FLORIDA — MOMENTS LATER

Victoriously, The Nagging Man steps out of the office with the CHECK in hand. He gets into his car and screeches off.

Even though The Nagging Man was heroic, I never want to rely on him again. Therefore, when booked on a job directly without an agent, I ask to be paid that same day of shoot. If they can't cough up payment the day of, that's a bad sign. A deal-breaker.

Famed rap duo Havoc and Prodigy from Mobb Deep once rapped, "Ain't no such thing as halfway crooks." True! And there's no such thing as halfway producers. He's either all producer or no producer at all. I warn actors ought to steer clear of these halfway crooks.

On the flipside, there are actor world experiences which are nothing short of awesome. I have managed to make some serious coin on certain gigs where I was compensated not only the day of the shoot, but on the back end as well with—every actor's favorite word—residuals. This is money the performer accrues each time a commercial, show, or movie is aired. It is essentially a steady income in the not-so-steady world of entertainment. These residuals are thanks to the Screen Actors Guild (SAG).

To this day I am still receiving checks in the mail from various union gigs I have done.

There was this Dodge commercial I did a few years back. It was to introduce the latest Dart model. It was an especially lucrative gig for me, as they were shooting both English and Spanish versions. I worked maybe two hours. I was portraying the car company's finance guy. It consisted of me putting on a suit, sitting at a desk arrogantly, and bilingually delivering one whole line. After being presented with info about new Dodge Dart's amazing features and low starting price, I replied, "You can't do that."! After a few easy takes where I said my line in two languages, I was on my way.

Two weeks later I received a check for around $1,200 which was for the actual shoot. That's known in the union world as the session fee. But that was just the beginning. My mug was going to be broadcasted nationally and every time that commercial aired, your boy got paid residuals. Ka-ching, ka-ching! Over the course of one year, I earned approximately $35,000. It was glorious gig. I get excited thinking about it, but the truth is this is only fair. Every time my image is used to sell a product, I should be compensated. Just as I have to pay my monthly bill as I keep using electricity, an actor should be compensated for the ongoing usage of their likeness.

On set for the Dodge Dart commercial. Circa 2015

Of course this isn't always the case, especially in Florida. The vast majority of the work I get is nonunion, so I kind of have my own personal standard of pay that I require in order to keep my hustle uniform and dignified.

Subject to change, here are my rates as a one-man union:

FILM / TV
1/2 Day Rate (Direct) $125.00
Day Rate (Direct) $200
1/2 Day Rate $200
Day Rate. $250.00

COMMERCIAL
1/2 Day Rate (Direct). $400
Day Rate (Direct). $700
1/2 Day Rate. $1,000.00
Day Rate. $2,000.00

*All rates are subject to change as the one-man union may be quite hard up for cash after blowing several stacks on a European vacation or stupidly on sneakers.

Ultimately your art is a business. Monetizing art is an ironic endeavor, especially as an actor. Because the need to do isn't easily satisfied. If you're a painter, you can simply whip out some paints, a canvas, and an easel and get to stroking. But an actor has to be granted access and then chosen. No matter how proactive you are, someone still needs to say yes. Why yes, you got the part! Of course, when one arrives to star status, you get to call the shots and choose your projects. But as a blue-collar actor like myself, you must be predisposed to compromises. We have to get in where we fit in, where we hope to fit in, or where we are allowed to fit in.

This is why we tend to be taken advantage of. Why we don't even bat an eye at a disparaging rate, or even work for free. After a few years of experience in the business, you learn to stand up for yourself, respect your time, and lobby more for a fair wage. Your time is worth money. Make sure they know that.

PET PROJECTS

"Success is not based on spontaneous
combustion; you have to light yourself on fire."
— Ralph Waldo Emerson

The above quote rings very true for those of us who work in the arts. The majority of actors I encounter are continually lighting themselves on fire. Many actors have side pursuits, but they remain within the realm of creativity. I am a writer. I've written several unproduced screenplays, as well as this very book. I have a penchant for venturing concepts and ideas, finding myself penning the occasional poem as well. With the mind of a poet who was raised on a whole lot of hip-hop, I also tend to write these poems as rhymes to beats so that would make me a rapper.

This is common. I have come across fellow actors who are also painters, fashion designers, writers, singers, musicians, stand-up comics, dancers, and the beat goes on. I believe actors have restless hearts by nature. We are continually yearning to give voice to our emotions. If we fail to vent, the more they accumulate and weigh on us. Festering. It's at this point that I douse myself in a combustible liquid and light a match, fanning the flames into action.

It's interesting that actors serve as vessels of characters, emotions, and stories that are generally the ideas of a third party. But we are also vessels for ourselves. Yeah, we can look pretty as fuck to personify some words on a screenplay, but we have our own ideas, damn it, our own fears, loves, and passions. And we act on all of this. There's no art more genuine to you than the art of being yourself.

Picture a struggling actor, schlepping across the city, sitting in traffic, fixing her hair, checking out her teeth in the vanity—all in the hopes of booking a commercial. She sends in casting tapes. (Even though tapes are long gone, the industry still refer to any kind of digital video submission as a tape.) The hope is that tape submission will result in getting three lines on some shitty web series. So much time and energy goes into giving life to somebody else's product or narrative. Why? The money? Maybe. But this is the life she enjoys, being on set, performing, and having others validate her talents. When she's not doing a career gig, she may find equal satisfaction in a pet project.

Not only are these pet projects therapy for the soul, but they could change your career trajectory. Let's take Matt Damon and Ben Affleck's little pet screenwriting project *Good Will Hunting*. A best-case scenario. Don't get me wrong; as young men these guys weren't exactly struggling. They were starring in indie hits and Hollywood misses. But back in the 90's they weren't household names by any stretch—that is, until they took home Oscars for best screenplay. And rightfully so. This gem of a film was once just a pet project like any other, a concept your restless heart kicks around and then fortunately decides to see through to fruition.

It probably began as a pet project that well-meaning friends think you crazy for undertaking, but will politely ask about every now and then. How's that whole screenplay thing going? Fast forward two years later. " Oh, yeah, I actually won an Oscar for it.

How do you like them apples?"

My rapping pet projects tend to have common themes: travel and history. The zeal I have for random places on this planet is in lockstep with the zeal I have for viewing places through a historical or nostalgic lens, and when I can blend these with my individuality, my rapper persona is 100% alive.

To highlight a few, I am particularly proud of "Bde Maka Ska," a song/video I made about Minneapolis, the city of my boyhood. Bde Maka Ska is the Native American name of the lake formerly called Calhoun. As a boy, I would spend countless fun-filled days at this lake. Upon planning my return to the city, as an adult in my 30's, I learned that the lake had been politically corrected by being re-named Bde Maka Ska. This seemed like such a Minneapolis thing to do, so that became the concept behind the song. "Bde Maka Ska" is retrospective music video that pays homage to the native people that once dwelled in the area. It's also about me, a man hopped on nostalgia, paying homage to who and where he was as a kid.

Heavier on my go-to location theme, I recently made a music video called "Christmas on South Beach." Some of my friends remarked that I went a little pop on this project, but my goal was to make it as bubble gum as I could. Come late November, we are bombarded by Christmas songs that celebrate the holiday in cold climates. "Christmas on South Beach" is the antithesis to this, a love letter to the city of Miami Beach and Dade County as a whole. The young woman in the video is Miami herself, a metaphor for a town that knows no winter and shines brightly all year even when the rest of the country is cold and gloomy.

Christmas on South Beach with Santa Claus and Jesus

Another common outlet for actors is stand-up comedy. In fact, I know a few of these funny folks. What a special talent to possess—to take a stage in front of perfect strangers and make them laugh. Eddie Murphy called his hit show Raw for a reason; stand-up comedy is as raw as entertainment gets. No frills, no filters, no razzle-dazzle, just a man (or woman) on a stage with a microphone,. Good comedians, equipped with ingenuity, can kill the crowd by breaking down life's monumental moments and rendering them trivial and ridiculous and universal. Remember that plenty of comedians used their joke-telling talents to kick down the gates of the Hollywood keepers, bringing their funny personas to the screens of our local cineplexes or living rooms. (Some of them pivoted into dramatic roles, really wowing us. Think of

Adam Sandler, Jenny Slate, Ben Stiller, and Mo'Nique.) Respect for the comedians!

My pet projects have not yet seen colossal success, but just being able to create is a blessing in itself. I could gush a whole book's worth about pet projects, because they nurture me. I need to have them. Just as you may and should. What is the end goal? Just to create and the process is valuable to one's heart. Some people climb mountains, I make rap videos (for now). Emerson made me do it, people.

Nurture your pet projects, whether you're a writer, a painter, a musician, or any other expressive entity. You'll be more enriched as a human for it. This in turn makes you more of an effective actor, since you are more in tune with yourself and your strengths.

TALENT

"The better the actor, the more stupid he is."
— Truman Capote

Actors on the job are referred to as *The Talent*. When I wasn't an actor, just a hacky-sack kicking, pimply face film student, I felt it was pompous to unequivocally deem all humans in front of a camera as *The Talent*. I wasn't alone. As our teacher was preparing us for a shoot day, one of the more bold pupils asked, "Uh, what if the actor sucks? Are they still the talent?"

"Yes, they are," the teacher replied.

Let us here both praise and poke fun at those that are good or bad, able to recall their lines or not, and hit their marks or not, feign an English accent or not, and show up on set no matter what, rain or shine. All hail The Talent.

Well into my 20's, upon landing my first commercial gig, I was now considered *The Talent*. However, I was resistant to that term initially. After a few projects under my belt, I finally accepted it. In fact, I proudly owned it. I have a higher calling and that matters. So here I am.

I am even learning to be treated like royalty. Thank you, Kenny the PA, for holding this umbrella over my freshly made-up face, in between takes. You are shielding my talented ass from the brutal beating of the sun. My appearance and my comforts take priority over everyone else's. Still feels weird, but that's acting.

EXT. COMMERCIAL SET - EARLY MORNING

ANDY, a newbie actor in his mid to late 20's, wayward in his ways, gets out of his 10-year-old Honda and makes his way to a bustling commercial set, past the trailers, toward the food truck.

> ANDY (VO)
> Here we go. It's showtime, baby.

After ordering his food, he turns to the picnic tables of the CREW, eating and socializing. Andy, feeling invisible, finds a seat on an empty table and begins eating.

Then moments later:

> KENNY THE PA (OS)
> Hey, are you my talent?

Andy peers up from his omelet.

> ANDY
> Uhh… No, I'm just one of the actors.

KENNY THE PA

Dude, you're talent. They need you in wardrobe.

ANDY

Oh. Right now?

KENNY THE PA

Does a bear shit in the woods? Yeah, now. Take your eggs with you.

Andy scarfs down what's left of his eggs and chugs his coffee.

KENNY THE PA

(into walkie)

Sending talent to wardrobe now.

Kenny shakes his head as Andy scurries to the trailers.

INT. WARDROBE TRAILER - MOMENTS LATER

WENDY, the wardrobe lady who feeds on stress, is working with her ASSISTANT, who steams and hangs clothes on a rack.

WENDY

Where the fuck is the talent? Jesus!

There's a KNOCK at the trailer door.

WENDY

Who knocks? Come in!

Andy enters.

ANDY

Good morning.

WENDY

Not exactly. Are you talent?

ANDY

Uhh.

WENDY

Uhh..? Yes or no?

ANDY

Yes! I am. I am the talent.

Wendy snatches a shirt and pants that the Assistant was steaming and hands it to Andy.

WENDY

Great, put this on. Go back there.

In the back of the trailer, Andy quickly strips down to his briefs. He looks directly in the mirror at his slender torso, then directly into his own eyes.

                    ANDY
                 (to himself)
          I'm the fuckin' talent.

He changes into wardrobe.

                                    FADE OUT:

Occasionally, but only occasionally, I get that beginner's feeling of not being *The Talent*. And sometimes I miss it. That feeling of just being *YOU* as you are on a set from call time to wrap. Not feeling the pressures of perfectly hitting your mark, knowing your lines, and looking your best. But just being behind the scenes and working, sweating, smoking cigarettes among the crew, cracking jokes about The Talent over walkie. Back when I was casting for Reality TV and poring over thousands of submissions to decide who would be *The Talent*, there was a liberation. It's a freedom that I now recognize in retrospect after being *The Talent*.

I've actually researched the origins of the term for about 30 seconds, Googling the question: Why are actors referred to as the talent?. There was nothing.

I was kinda hoping to find some article that harks back to Hollywood's Golden Age. A contemporary account about some insecure, yet larger-than-life actress, a stunning beauty with blonde, shimmering hair who was in dire need of some ass kissing.

Ms. So and So just wouldn't cut it upon arrival to set. No, she demanded to be referred to as the one and the only Talent. Perhaps there was argument about a line in a script. She wanted to change it, but the producer defended the writer of the script. At this point she erupted, announcing that she's the Talent. She was the end-all and be-all—and if anyone disagrees, she will quit the project. From that point on, everyone agreed to call her the Talent on set and on every other movie thereafter. The term stuck and spread to other actors, and due time to every other fussy actor. Sure, the above is a random speculation, but you being The Talent is a fact. So what are you going to do with it?

Being dressed and made up to be Ronald McDonald, while floating in a pool and sipping from a Subway cup takes real talent.

GOOD
MOURNING

"All the art of living lies in the fine mingling
of letting go and holding on."
— Havelock Ellis

As we now know, an actor's calendar should be flexible. One must be able to drop whatever's happening to report to a set or an audition. The show must go on. It always does. And this applies to even the bleakest of situations, those sudden or not-so-sudden tragedies that smack us into a different reality. Specifically, the loss of a loved one.

Soon after completion of the first draft of this book, my brother Alex died. It happened out of nowhere. My family was given no warning to brace for impact. Some say this type of loss hits you like a ton a bricks. For me, it was the feeling of a ton of bricks recklessly ripped from the foundation of your heart. Leaving nothing but shambles. It's an emotional injury for which there is no vaccine, prosthetic, or surgeon. The only medication, if you're lucky to have it, is the support of loving family and friends, coming together while all suffering from the same condition. Misery does indeed love company, especially when that company is loving.

(I pause and meditate, a common ritual of my mourning, and kiss the ring which once belonged to my brother.)

My brother Alex was the guy responsible for my love of movies. He also laid the groundwork for many other aspects of my identity. He was nine years my senior. When I was a youngster in the mid 80's, Alex turned me on to early rap, blasting cuts by The Beastie Boys, L.L. Cool J, and Run-DMC. I was granted a license to ill and was hooked. Then he switched genres, taking off the A Tribe Called Quest record and laying on some Prince, Smiths, or Bob Marley. I remember him coming home from epic concerts wearing t-shirts from Public Enemy or Dead Kennedys.

As far as films go, Alex brought classics to my attention, from *Star Wars* to *Apocalypse Now*. He explained about the directors and how some of them are more intrepid than others: Lynch, The Coen Brothers, Coppola, Scorsese. I believe his favorite film of all time was the original dystopian classic *Mad Max*. (Hope I got that right, Alex.)

He was also uber-stylish. As a teenager, he wore outfits that were carefully curated ensembles that really reflected culture, the era, and his rebellious individualism. Cool. You get it. I'll bring the brotherly gushing to a halt now.

Alex's physical presence has departed. Yet I'm still here, living with an even greater sense of him and his spirit. Maybe there is someone you know who has affected your life as Alex has affected mine. If so, I encourage you to thank them and show them love while they're still around.

Back to the regular scheduled programming: acting career advice.

Be warned: this profession accepts no excuse when it comes to showing up and working. I was booked on a Mercedes commercial soon after Alex's passing. But immersed in grieving I had totally forgotten. That is, until I was reminded by the wardrobe department. They called while I was bawling like a baby on the other line, discussing arrangements with the funeral parlor. I clicked over and the wardrobe lady knew immediately that something wasn't right, asking if everything was ok before checking to see if I had a solid blue button-down shirt. I had to call her back after the funeral chat.

There I was, destroyed, freshly brotherless, choking on tears, and going over my sizes and inventory of grey, black, and blue tops for a fucking Mercedes commercial. In a regular person job, after the loss of a loved one, they grant you a week break at the very least. It's not even a question and you'll be paid. Not us actors. Sure we can bail, but you get a rep for being flakey. When the industry gossip starts, the part about you canceling because of a death in the family will get lost in the retelling. Oh yeah, and you'll be earning absolutely nothing. Sorry for your loss and your loss.

I couldn't really worry too much about any of this though. I ended up reporting to set four days after Alex's passing to be in some silly car commercial. Why? Well, as the date crept up, I kept asking myself two questions. Can I even keep it together on the set? And what would Alex want? The third question was unspoken: Am I even an actor?

God, I sure hope so – since I'm one chapter away from completing a book on the subject.

And as far as what my brother Alex would want, as I imagine any loved one gleaming at us from the afterlife would, he'd encourage me to keep on with doing me, get that money, and not to wallow in the sorrow of his absence (for too long).

As I arrived to set, I suddenly was overcome by an immense feeling, the likes of which I have never felt. It's as if I was gone like Alex and I had just returned, back from the dead, back into life, which was there all along. I felt as if I had emerged from the wreckage. Yet I still felt that the wreckage remained within.

Here on set, not a soul knew my brother nor what I had just gone through. My acting kicked in long before the director yelled action. That is, I greeted crew and fellow talent. I enthusiastically made a beeline for the coffee at crafty. It was noon by now, so the java had already cooled down. Cool coffee in hand, forced smile pasted on, I entered the wardrobe and make-up trailer with a cheery "Hello, people!"

The wardrobe woman, who still suspected something was amiss, again asked me if everything was OK. I was forced to divulging the news, while managing to keep the tear ducts reined in. She responded with genuine empathy, having lost a sibling some years back. We had work to do. I was supposed to bring clothes to try on, but I had spaced it.

Typically a wardrobe person would be livid, but this time I got a pass. And this wardrobe woman was a pro, her own arsenal of apparel at the ready. Then I was handed off to make-up. The make-up woman applied foundation under my sleepless, cried-out eyes, which were fixed on hers. Before handing me off to production, she noticed a necklace around my neck. My brother's ring was hanging from it. She reminded me that a Mercedes owner would never wear something like that, so I took it off and shoved it into my pocket. The make-up woman then offered to wear it while I worked. A blessing. Whenever she would retouch me or pat my sweaty face, I'd glance at the ring as it contentedly dangled around her neck.

Then it was time to meet the director, the AD. I was introduced to my faux family, which consisted of a wife, a talented actor whom I've seen on TV and at many auditions, a cutie-pie six-year-old daughter, and my son, a young theater actor from Orlando. The dog was a grey, long-hair spitzer kind of pooch, which was way too fluffy to be in working in the Miami Summer. And the star was there too: our brand new Mercedes, state-of-the-art, SUV.

We were directed to enter the car with smiles and excitement. Then I would press an icon on the dashboard's smart display and look back confidently at my kids and dog. We did that a few times.

After a few takes, the AD asked me to look happier. Right, happier. But, I wanted to say, my head is not in a happy mode right now. In fact, my heart is breaking. But I'm an actor; I am paid to make believe. In fact, I was giving a helluva performance that day; I was smiling when I felt like crying.

I thought back to childhood and grade school at Kenwood Elementary in Minneapolis, MN. After getting snagged for some kind of shenanigans, I would be scolded and sent to the principal's office. Up until the third grade, as the teacher would fill out the pass of shame, I'd cry. It was automatic and embarrassing. By fourth grade, I'd learned to stiffen my upper lip, hold back the tears, and go to the principal's office like a man. Maybe this was the skill I was using now to keep the waterworks from flowing.

Aside from the make-up and wardrobe gals, I kept the dark news to myself.

After the car entry shots, we all moved to the beach. Oh, the joy! This portion of the shoot was even more difficult as the scene called for beach fun. Playing on the sand with my children, laughing with them, chasing the dog, and hugging my wife. It was excruciating. But I delivered.

While my heart was grieving, my body was giving its all as an actor to sell the Mercedes-Benz GLC SUV. After the shoot wrapped, the makeup woman gently placed the necklace with the ring back around my neck. That prompted a smile—a genuine one. I realized the old cliché holds true: the show must go on.

I got in my Chevy Equinox and cried myself all the way the home.

FADE OUT

"Nothing happens unless we first dream."
— Carl Sandburg

Way back, at the turn of the 21st century, I was just an underweight college kid in an oversized sweatshirt sitting in a desk in the back of a screenwriting class. At the end of the course, the teacher randomly chose a couple scripts to read aloud. When I saw mine, *A Life in a Day*, plucked from the stack, I lit up with delight. This was a first for me. Up to that point, I have never had my work read publicly. I had never had an audience that didn't consist only of my mother.

The story tracks the life of an ardent art critic named Daniel Seasons who, by symbolism, lives out the course of his entire lifetime within one day. The hero springs out of bed in the morning, rides his bike past a flower stand, then meets a girl named Summer. Things heat up, but then begin to cool off as the hero's buddy warns him of Summer's cold side and to tread lightly with her. SPOILER ALERT: Daniel actually ends up dying at the end—or does he?

As the teacher read, I noticed with a distinct pride that he was reading with gusto, and that the class that was intently listening. There were even a couple chuckles along the way. It dawned on me that this is what it's like to get your ideas in front of an audience. I was beaming. For a while, anyway.

However, at the second to last page of this ten-page piece, the teacher paused. He looked at me, sighed, then continued to read the ending with a tad less enthusiasm. As the class was dismissed, he took me aside.

INT. FULL SAIL UNIVERSITY — MORNING — CR. 2000

Early millennium FILM STUDENTS gather Their books and file out of a classroom. The TEACHER eyes one kid in particular on the way out, ANDY — skinny as rail, in a white Polo HAT.

>   **TEACHER**
>   Andrew, not so bad.

>   **ANDY**
>   Yeah, thanks for picking it.

>   **TEACHER**
>   You had me there. You know, you
>   had us all there -- that is,
>   until the ending.

> **ANDY**
>
> So you didn't like the ending?

> **TEACHER**
>
> Not for a second, kiddo. You
> got lazy. Didn't you?

> **ANDY**
>
> I mean I had to end it somehow.

Teacher peers over the rim of his glasses.

> **TEACHER**
>
> If there's one thing you take
> away from this class. It's this
> lesson: don't end your stories
> with your hero waking up from
> a dream.

FADE OUT:

Don't end stories with your hero waking up from a dream. There was some truth to what he said. I admit that laziness inspired me to squeak out that ending. I needed to finish the assignment so I could hit the town and get white-boy-wasted at ten-cent beer night.

Apparently it's quite common among amateur writers to begin a story with the main character waking up. (By the way, nobody comes close to Pee-wee Herman's wake-up scene in Tim

Burton's "Pee-wee's Big Adventure." If you're going to use a cliché, knock it out of the park. #classic.) Cliché two: End a story with the hero waking up from a dream.

But I had committed both clichés and my reaming out was justified. Sorry, teach. The whole it-was-all-a-dream (RIP Biggie) ending is such an easy place to arrive as a new-jack writer who's not committed (yet) to being profound or original. He just wants to suck down some cheap suds. Yep, the college experience often gets in the way of good work.

Shortly after graduating, I rewrote that ending, eventually turning it into an actual film as mentioned in chapter one. And this time, instead of a dream, Daniel wakes up from a deep reverie inspired by a painting. After his unfortunate death, the camera dollies back from his lifeless body, dissolving into a painting of that last frame. We are now in an art gallery, where Daniel is very much alive, but just snapping out of a long observation of the painting. Daniel Seasons is an art critic, after all, and I figured it would be cool if he approves of paintings by physically experiencing what the artist endured to create the piece in the first place.

I wonder what discerning Daniel Seasons would think of my art as an actor. What I've been able to pull off, and lack thereof. Is my heart really in it? I think he would turn his nose up at my commercial work, approve of my film and TV work, and applaud my personal projects. But as I've laid out over these previous 100-plus pages, I love the process, the sets, the people, the industry, the castings, the techniques, and the excitement of developing an even more fruitful future in this business. Hopefully Daniel Seasons would approve of that too.

When we are fledgling artists in college, one of life's grand ironies is that teachers tend to steer us away from the pedestrian. But once we get into the real world, we are no longer students. We are human adults. And being an adult means making compromises for survival. We're expected to fill our bank account. That may mean letting go of certain virtues you may hold in high esteem, and exchange them for a big, fat check. Actors continuously deal with this dilemma. We have to take what we can get in that journey along that uncertain career road. And who knows where it might lead us? Maybe to a place where we can play among the elite, where we have the luxury of picking and choosing what we want to do. In the meantime, until we reach the promised land, we roll with the artistic compromises. We pull for the profound, fall short more often than not, and promise ourselves to try harder the next time. All the while, we are filling our pockets with needed cash while striving to fill our hearts with needed satisfaction.

You are an actor. This means you are a hired gun loaded with emotions. You're a pro at admiring non-existent beautiful sunsets and bursting into laughter or tears in response to absolutely nothing at all.

You are an actor, possessing plenty of love on tap. You're ready to serve it up for picture-perfect strangers at the drop of a dime. You're a little off beat, but always on time for the most turbulent of schedules. You, you, and you are all actors, beaming in headshots, scrambling for attention at your next gig, rehearsing yourself. Cursing yourself. Checking yourself means also occasionally checking yourself out in the monitor of the closed-circuit security system at the local Walgreens. Hamming it up. It's a life. A choice.

It's a life you are fortunate to pursue, tenaciously, all the way across the city, the state, the country, the calendar, and the world. You are an actor, striving for a living, recognition, or stardom. I know you and your world. Because I am also an actor—even if I still have trouble saying that very statement aloud: I am an actor. It helps when we are together, fellow actors, propping up each other's sagging confidence, commiserating over a failed audition, gossiping about a lunatic director, sharing awry experiences from set. I need you, the actor, the friend, to remind me that I am an actor as well.

And even when there isn't a camera or production crew in site, no lines from a script to memorize and deliver, no calls from agents, no castings to attend, we'd still be at it. Acting. No matter what day job, no matter what task, we'd still be cast members in the show called life. But damn it, we'd get star billing.

We are the stars of our very own lives. We are actors. It's who we are. Might was well get paid for it.

I will not end this book by waking up from a dream. That would be lazy and a total disservice to you, the reader. Let's land this plane by remaining in the dream. Because the dream is everything. Wherever you are, whenever you are, whoever you are, don't try waking up from that dream, fellow actor. Because it's that dream that keeps us awake. A dream so close, it's hovering just over the horizon of our hearts. The dream that is always pumping through our veins, lubricating our lives and our drive to continue to be who we are. It's a dream from which we should never awake. That's life. So, knock 'em dead—or alive—dreamers.

ABOUT THE AUTHOR

Andy Guze got his start in show business in 2002 behind the camera, from production work to casting. He finally focused his career solely on acting in 2010.

Since then, he has landed principle roles on scores of commercials —regional, national, and international. Top commercials include brands like Lexus, Subway, Hilton, Walmart, and Dodge—one of which took home an Emmy.

Andy has appeared in several shorts and feature-length movies that have appeared on the festival circuit, including Make Love Great Again which was picked up by HBO.

Andy has also been a guest star on TV series in both English and Spanish. His work can be seen currently streaming on platforms such as Blackpills, Amazon, and Netflix.

andyguze@gmail.com
Instagram: @andyguze
Twitter: @andyguze
www.andyguze.com

Made in the
USA
Middletown, DE